STEPH & DOM'S
guide to life

STEPH & DOM'S
guide to life

Steph & Dom Parker

CORONET

First published in Great Britain in 2015 by Coronet
An imprint of Hodder & Stoughton
An Hachette UK company

First published in paperback in 2016

1

Copyright © Stephanie and Dominic Parker 2015
Photography by Mark Harrison
Text consultation by Stephen Morrison

The right of Stephanie and Dominic Parker to be identified as the Author
of the Work has been asserted by them in accordance with the Copyright,
Designs and Patents Act 1988.

A CIP catalogue record for this title is available from the British Library

Paperback ISBN: 978 1 473 62064 3
Ebook ISBN: 978 1 473 62062 9

Typeset in Garamond 12/17pt by Born Group, London

Printed and bound in Italy by Graphicom

Hodder & Stoughton policy is to use papers that are natural, renewable
and recyclable products and made from wood grown in sustainable
forests. The logging and manufacturing processes are expected to conform
to the environmental regulations of the country of origin.

Hodder & Stoughton Ltd
Carmelite House
50 Victoria Embankment
London EC4Y 0DZ

www.hodder.co.uk

To our parents and children

Contents

Introduction

Hi, Steph and Dom here . . . yes that's right, the posh couple from *Gogglebox*. We're here to tell you about this nifty little book we've done. In handy reference form the book contains our unique take on how to get the most out of pretty much everything life throws at you. Now, before you think to yourself 'Doesn't a book have to be more than one page long to actually be a book?' we'd like to reassure you we've learnt loads actually! Admittedly we've learnt most of it by accident . . . but the point is, we're sharing it with you!

Through the medium of hilarity we'll show you everything from how to make an Irish coffee without having a mental breakdown to learning how you and your partner can grow young together and endure more fun than you ever thought possible. Anyway, it's a bloody useful little thing with all the wisdom we've collected over the years – so sit back, pour yourself a drink and let us be your booze consultants, your style gurus, your pub lunch professionals and your maverick marriage counsellors. Chin chin!

– Steph and Dom x

The Monopoly of Monogamy:

How to Get Everything Out of Your Relationship

The secret to a good relationship is this: be two very different people . . . with a lot in common. There's nothing worse than seeing couples who have morphed into each other, with the same stooped gait. Start like that and you'll end up even looking like each other. Seriously, it happens! The Proclaimers are actually man and wife! No I'm joking, they're not . . . but moving on.

You need two different people in a relationship, two people who absolutely adore each other and make each other bloody laugh. Because when the ground shifts, and mark my words, it bloody well will shift – seriously, just when you think you've got it sussed, something will knock you for six – you'll need two different minds to stay on the ride. So here's everything we've learnt about getting and *keeping* it on. Enjoy!

– Steph

ANECDOTE FATIGUE

The phrase 'familiarity breeds contempt' is never truer than when applied to the anecdotes you and your partner will continue to chuck out like a juke box until the end of your days. Even the best stories, the most fun stories in the world, will feel tired to your partner the thousandth time around. A common error when sensing anecdote fatigue is to try and beef up the anecdote your partner is reiterating in order to make it more interesting. This will only convey desperation and confusion for the recipient.

Remember instead, that though the story may no longer be funny to *you* about your partner writing the 'C' word in shaving foam on the bonnet of the newlyweds' Rolls-Royce, only to find that it burnt into the paintwork rendering the slur irremovable, it is still a very funny story and will be funny to those new to it. With this in mind, it is better to take yourself away from your partner's story and just let them get on with it. Use the time to have a cigarette if you smoke or to straighten the pasta in your kitchen if you have OCD.

BAD PATCHES

No matter how good things are in your relationship,

you will from time to time feel like your partner is just causing you more problems than they are helping to solve. This can be a sudden realisation or one that grows over a period of time. The worst thing to do when suddenly overcome with the feeling that 'things are a bit shit' is to angrily vocalise your thoughts. This will cause damage which may be irreparable (see *The 'D' Word*).

Instead the best thing to do is to relax, in the same way a new-born kitten does when it is lifted by the mum cat by the back of its neck. Let the current of the bad patch carry you; it will soon put you down and you will be able to assess things with a clearer head. If, however, the bad patch is becoming a bad allotment (e.g. there is a lot more of it than you initially thought) then the first thing to do is check your own recent behaviour before challenging your partner, because nobody gets out of a bad patch by continuing to be a 'bit of a twat'.

BE ALL OF YOURSELVES

In an intimate relationship there are always two personalities. All too often, however, these two personalities will decide which is the stronger of the two. The stronger will then hog most of the relationship, in the same way the big wheel on a penny-farthing hogs most of the bike (the person considered to have the lesser personality would then receive the consolation prize of being the tiny wheel at the back).

This approach to a relationship is as moribund as the penny-farthing bicycle itself. A good relationship involves two equally sized personalities and both of you should get to be all of yourselves. Staying with the penny-farthing metaphor, it is important to note that the front-wheel personality should not shrink down to the size of the runt-wheel personality. Instead the smaller wheel should be able to grow to the size of the big wheel. We would like to apologise for the overstretching of the penny-farthing metaphor. We assure you that if we refer to cycles in any way for the remainder of this heading, we will give you a free drink if you stay at our hotel. But in a nutshell, one's game can always be upped but must never be downed.

A relationship is not a competition where there is an outright winner. Let your personalities be as massive as they actually are. You are not determined by minor and major. You are determined by a thread that runs through you both and is unbroken (a bit like the metal chassis of a bike. Ooof!).

BLIND DATES

Many of you may already know that we met on a blind date. So we're pro blind dates to the max. Our situation was slightly unique, however, since it turned out we had met ten years previously (which gave the date a sort of *When Harry Met Sally* impetus to it although our scene in the diner wasn't quite as noisy). So ours was not so much a blind date as a 'slightly visually impaired' date.

Real blind dates are simply a lottery, even if they've been set up by friends or colleagues. They are like a fruit machine where you only get one spin. The likelihood of getting three cherries first time is slim, and if you don't then you have to move on to another fruit machine completely. And remember, please gamble with love responsibly.

BEDROOMS (SEPARATE)

Since sanity is vital to surviving a relationship, it is important both partners receive adequate rest. So when it comes to sleeping, 'get another room'. There is no merit in having your circadian rhythm disturbed by your partner throwing themselves about like they're losing at judo. Or shouting 'SPICE

GIRLS ARE IN MY CAR' in their sleep. Having separate rooms will not infringe upon your sex life. Especially if matters are addressed shortly after lunch. Uneventful and fulfilling sleep is a basic necessity for a happy marriage and must never be compromised!

CHATTING UP (WOMEN)

These methods could work on men also, and could be deployed by women on men, women on women or men on men. We're just putting them under the women heading because we've witnessed a measure of success here. Generally, ordering a bottle of Champagne to be sent to the table of the object of your affection is a good 'in'. It is a generous and flattering statement which would give any recipient a bit of a buzz. Once your expensive gesture of flattery is complete, remain calm, and don't be pushy. If there was ever any chance of you both uniting for eternity, another nice thing to do is to approach the woman in question and say, 'Excuse me, I hope you don't mind me interrupting, nothing in it, but I just had to say, "You look simply stunning."' Then get on with your respective evenings.

NOTE: When 'chatting up people', try not to have pustules, cankers, weeping sores or a horn coming out of your head like a rhino, as we imagine any of these may be counterproductive to the venture.

CHATTING UP (MEN)

Once again this approach would readily work along the whole gamut of gender and sexuality but we just think it's hotter if a woman does it to a guy. There, we said it! The following simple win-win approach provides an arena for light flirtatious conversation as well as an easy get-out clause. Move away from your girlfriends, approach the man you are interested in and say, 'Excuse me, could you help settle an argument? My friends think you're actually from (CURRENT CITY) whereas I think you're just visiting.' Your mark will be immediately flattered and energised by this fresh approach. And by 'your mark' we mean the object of your affection. We are not suggesting all men are called Mark.

NOTE: It is important that you name the *actual* current city you are in during your dalliance with Mark and not say 'brackets current city close brackets', as this will give the game away immeasurably.

CONSIDERING YOUR PARTNER IS NOT A WEAKNESS

All too often people in relationships are chastised by their friends whenever they are unable to make a decision without their partners. When you become a genuinely true partnership there are decisions that you shouldn't take without the other's input. When it comes to making any decision you feel is a big one, think Queen Victoria, e.g. think in the 'We' sense rather than the 'I' sense (but do not go around holding an orb, creating a repressive moralistic atmosphere everywhere you go).

COUPLES' MASSAGE

This is largely ineffective, because no matter how good the massage you are receiving, you will find it difficult to relax. This is because you will be facing your partner while someone younger and lither than you caresses their lower back, often flying dangerously close to their backside. Couples' massages can also be expensive. As well as the initial outlay, you will be expected to pay any garage bills incurred by your partner's masseuse after you are caught keying their Saab.

DON'T SWEAT THE SMALL STUFF

Magnifying any irritating foibles your partner may

demonstrate is a total waste of time. You can adapt to survive almost anything pithy that they do. You will only ever have as much as a 98 per cent perfect relationship and pushing for the extra 2 per cent will only cause you to lose what you already have. To put this point into context, as well as show how blatantly obvious it is to determine a shortfall in character, we recommend you carry out the exercise below and over the page.

EXERCISE: Separate the following personal shortcomings into 'Minor Foibles' and 'Major Concerns':

Jam hands

Sniffing

Unkempt eyebrows

Gambling addiction

Failing to place celebrities' names on TV

Untidiness

Lateness

Over-consulting with waiters

Dependency on heroin

Whistling

Clumsiness

Using an axe to kill penguins

Bath overspill

Snoring

Obsession with ZZ Top

Repeatedly kicking livestock down a spiral staircase

Arson

DRASTIC HAIRCUTS

It is advisable that any changes in your hairstyle that you wish to undertake should be discussed with your partner beforehand. Failing to do so will cause them to sulk for roughly a year (or about the same time it takes to regrow six inches of hair). There is no known excuse for skipping a partner consultation prior to getting short hair.

DRESSING FOR A FIRST DATE

We have never worried about what to wear for a date, let alone for our first date. In fact, on our first date (after the blind date) one of us simply wore a towel, so let's just say it was a resounding success.

ENGAGEMENT RINGS

To the best of our understanding and experience, the following steps should help take the pain out of obtaining a suitable engagement ring.

1. Meet jeweller friend and describe preferred dimensions of ring.
2. Ensure fiancée is happy with how ring will look.
3. Haemorrhage cash.
4. Wait roughly two weeks.
5. Collect and marvel at ring. Assume fiancée has gone a little bit quiet because she is lost for words.
6. Get drunk at a function and realise fiancée is upset.
7. Press fiancée about what is upsetting her until she says as kindly as possible, 'It's not big enough.'
8. Confirm fiancée's statement was about diamond ring and not something else.
9. Breathe sigh of relief.
10. Return to jeweller friend, explaining plans to super-size main diamond in ring.
11. Discover diamond cannot be altered due to bespoke nature and that entirely new diamond must be obtained.
12. Remember to give fiancée the nickname 'Gollum' in the hope it will stick.
13. Agree to obtainment of new 'one ring'.
14. Haemorrhage cash at more alarming rate.
15. Wait two weeks.

16. Receive the 'one ring' together, informing fiancée old one has been sold.
17. Just before wedding, present fiancée with surprise gift of old diamond attached to gold necklace.
18. Receive lifelong supply of 'blow job coupons' in return.
19. Realise these coupons are largely worthless (see *Sexual Currency*).
20. Enjoy an amazing life together along with new fun upbeat anecdote about hellish engagement ring acquisition.

FLOWERS

Many people believe that any aspect of a relationship can be improved by the giving of flowers. In fact the giving of flowers actually causes more problems than it solves. The moment the intended recipient sees their partner advancing with finely wrapped blooms they will immediately think, 'OH GOD, WHAT HAVE THEY DONE?!'

HOW TO ARGUE WITH YOUR PARTNER

The answer to this is as simple as it is profane: 'Have massive ding-dongs . . . then wait to calm down.'

JOINT ACCOUNTS

Just as beds must be separate in a good marriage, bank accounts must be 'joint'. There is nothing either more saddening or more embarrassing than seeing a couple squabble over whose turn it is to buy the gin, dinner, petrol or sex. It is our opinion that when you made your vows you agreed to share everything, regardless of its value. Sharing of razors, however, should be considered wisely.

KISSING (IN PRIVATE)

Many things are often described as 'being better than sex' (tax refunds, chocolate, seeing a dog do a double take), yet nothing really beats kissing. This is because the mouth is one of the most erotic parts of the body and kissing your partner should almost definitely be the highlight of your day. Remember that your partner's tongue is your tongue's dance partner so it is advisable to develop a number of dances to keep them on their toes, e.g. a Viennese Waltz for a lazy Saturday lunchtime or the Charleston if you are clock watching.

MARRIAGE

When the institution of marriage was first created,

the average lifespan of a human was thirty-five
years. This may make marriage sound hugely
outdated given that back then, when people said
'till death us do part', they really meant 'till we
live to the age where we decide to start framing all
our art prints'. However, marriage is not about the
institution. It is about the person you love.
Therefore marriage is an important statement,
but not an essential one, so never marry out of an
obligation to tradition; marry only if you are deeply
in love with 'the one'.

NOTICING HAIRDOS

Unless your partner chooses something particularly
drastic at the salon (see *Drastic Haircuts*), the chances
are you will fail to notice their hairdo. This is because,
generally, the difference between your partner's pre-
salon and after-salon hair is roughly the same as the
formational change of a stalagmite over a period of
exactly one week. For this reason it is well worth getting
a copy of your partner's salon visitation schedule. Using
this, you should then phone the salon while your partner
is there and ask to speak to them. When they are on
the phone simply say, 'Your hair looks wonderful by the

way.' Then simply hang up. You have then successfully fulfilled your obligation to notice your partner's hair.

PROPOSING

Never propose to anyone unless you are certain of the answer. If you are certain the answer will be 'no' we wouldn't recommend proposing either, largely because if you do so with an expensive diamond ring, there is a very strong chance you will not get it back. You do not need a ring at this stage anyway. Once certain the answer will be 'yes' and provided you yourself are happy with the prospect of being together forever, the best thing is to park it completely and get on with your life.

We cannot stress enough how important it is to just stop worrying about proposing. This is because when it is the right time to propose it is the right time to propose. It does not matter where you are, what you are both wearing. You could be in the knicker section in M&S when it just pours out of you. Don't get down on one knee either. That was only fashionable back when a charger was a horse and not an elusive plug for your smartphone. As long as you take yourself by surprise, you'll take your partner by surprise and, in so doing, will have furnished them with a good story to tell everyone.

NOTE: It is perfectly normal for the proposee to revert to sarcastic comedy or mock underwhelming during a proposal; something like: 'Is that it?!' This is their way of saying, 'This is awesome! But get down on one knee!'

PROXIMITY OVEREXPOSURE

Cohabiting with someone for an extended period of time will result in their getting under your feet occasionally. This will even occur if you live in a Lutyens-designed seventeen-bedroom luxury hotel. The best thing to do is to complain about it before proceeding with your routine. However, before you revert to loudly stating something like 'Why are you everywhere I need to be?' be prepared for the retort, 'Well, did it ever occur to you that you might be everywhere I want to bloody be?' Some common symptoms of proximity overexposure to your partner are a heightened awareness of throat clearing or breathing, or how annoying they sound while eating an apple.

PUBLIC DISPLAYS OF AFFECTION

There are laws against these in some countries, which sounds, let's face it, a bit much. It would hardly seem right to find yourself in prison and at the point where all the lags ask 'What you in for?' and your answer is 'I spooned my wife on a bandstand.' There are many types of affection, many more extreme than others, yet all of them have their pitfalls, so read on.

DRY HUMPING
Just no.

HOLDING HANDS
This is perfectly harmless and highly recommended. Not only will it enable you to stop your partner entering shops and spending money but it will continually reassure your connection. Holding hands can make a couple seem a bit woolly if not relaxed so try to do it casually and not have a face like you're a delighted child holding a balloon at a fair.

KISSING

It is not uncommon to be overwhelmed by the beauty of your partner and have a sudden urge to kiss them in public. This is totally fine, you're only human and they are totally hot. However, don't peck them repetitively, as this can look needy. Just go for one meaningful kiss, and make sure the kiss is set to mute for God's sake.

LEANING/LOUNGING

Sitting in a park with your partner's massive head on your lap while you waft them with a dock leaf is fine, romantic even (except for the dock leaf part). If you are outdoors, however, be aware of forces that may cause you to suddenly have to get up and move, e.g. bad weather, bad busking or Seagull attacks. Gentlemen should be particularly aware of this before committing to developments in the trouser department.

SNOGGING

This depends on where you are. A dimly lit dance floor would be fine. A church or hospital waiting room would not. If you are going to go for it, then just go for it. Just remember not to lose track of your week too much.

PUSHING THE ENVELOPE

Persistently repeating an action that you know is annoying your partner is one of the best things about being in a relationship. In fact, the level of enjoyment in pushing your partner's buttons is directly proportional to the amount of trouble you're currently in. Repeating a stupid noise, grape throwing, or water pistol abuse are all tried and tested ways of sending your partner 'batshit with rage'.

Remember that your partner will always be like America when it comes to retaliation so be prepared for a hugely disproportionate violent retort to whatever antic you have perpetrated. So two sprays of a water pistol will equal roughly two paddling pools' worth of water emptied over you sometime later that day, and when you are least expecting it.

The only way to counter partner retaliation is to theatricalise whatever annoyance you plan to visit on them in the hope that they will laugh so much at how much effort you have put in. For example, if you are planning to blow BBQ soot into your sunbathing partner's face, the best way to do it is to take your top off, mark your face like a tribal hunter and advance stealthily up the garden towards them with the soot ready to blow in your flat hand (and a raised pretend-spear in the form of a garden cane in the other).

RENEWING VOWS

Honestly? What on earth is that all about?! As far as we are concerned a vow is just that, and needs no further affirmation. The act of renewing wedding vows is deemed as pointless as contacting Deed Poll to confirm your name is Barry (provided your name *really* is Barry). When saying 'I do' – during the part of the wedding ceremony when you are supposed to, of course – you have then made the vow as permanent as a turmeric stain on an unvarnished farm table. So, instead of having an official renewal of vows, just have the bloody party and toast your success at getting this far!

ROMANCE ON A BUDGET

You do not really need money to be romantic. In fact some of the most romantic memories are often a result of 'making do' and being as adventurous as you both can be with whatever given situation.

Romance requires a concept, a location, an instance of planning and simplicity. So, finding you've missed the train in Whitstable, then choosing to stay on the beach with fish and chips and wine, would fit the bill brilliantly and we highly recommend it.*

*An impromptu date such as the above would only be cheap if you lived in or around the Kent area. If you were in Glasgow, for example, travelling all the way to Whitstable for haddock and Merlot near some waves would be entirely non-cost-effective.

ROWING IN PUBLIC

Rowing in public is often referred to as 'washing your dirty linen in public'. However, this is wildly inaccurate as the comparison would suggest that the couple are actually improving something, e.g. sanitising something unclean. In reality, rowing in public is the equivalent of fouling yourself in public in front of the opposite sex, and it should be quite clear that this is something nobody wants to do (see *Unisex Loos*).

SENSING FUN

While growing young together is certainly the way forward, you may at times find that the 'flying by the seat of your pants' approach may turn a few heads, especially if you are writing off upholstery in the process. This is because although nearly everyone enjoys a bit of a laugh, many will believe there is a time and a place for it. This is completely true, of course. There is a time and a place for fun. The time is as soon as possible. The place is wherever *you* are.

In the same way a salmon goes out of its way upriver to get its lady salmon, so too should a couple make a considerable effort to have fun. Having a sense of fun means that fun can be sensed – you will know it instantly: it smells of insubordination and mischief and once you pick up the scent you should make a beeline for it. While it is important to go out of your way to have fun, you should never go out of your way to try and be funny. Funny is the by-product of fun, so aiming straight for funny will just make you tired and possibly something of a twat.

SENSITIVE BIRTHDAYS

Birthday cards which cite 'Happy Birthday Old Fart' etc. should never be given, as they may, by an off-chance, cause a midlife crisis to the recipient. This could then result in them arriving at a lunch meeting with a pierced ear and pony-tail, boasting a kaleidoscope of sexual conquests. Cards should always be humorous, sometimes rude, but never too close to the truth! So, the next time you find yourself looking for a card for an overweight family member, go for the funny animal photos for fear of having an offensive one returned to you. References to their endless abuse of alcohol are perfectly acceptable and almost par for the course.

SEX GIGGLES

Widely renowned as the most fun of all the sexual pitfalls, laughing at your partner during sex is regarded as a win-win situation given all the outcomes available.

Outcome 1: The sex stops but the laughter continues. A great evening is had by all.

Outcome 2: The laughter acts as a welcome intermission before the more serious second half of the show commences.

Outcome 3: Neither the laughter nor the sex go away, to the point where a synaesthesia of hilarity and arousal is obtained, and where nobody can tell if falling off a bed together is piss-pant funny or erotic.

SEXUAL CURRENCY

Never accept the promise of a sexual favour from your partner (or indeed anyone else) as payment for anything. The 'usual bet' will never come to light. Trying to get your partner to honour something rude they scrawled on a piece of paper several weeks ago is like trying to pay a bar bill with Monopoly money. Quite simply put, you cannot bank a BJ.

SMELL

This sense is thought to be something of a sheriff when it comes to carnal law. Indeed, most people's olfactory diagnosis will be the biggest factor in determining if someone is *hot* or indeed *not*. Fascinatingly, however, the sense of smell actually shuts down somewhat in humans when they are aroused, which makes a lot of sense really, since we'd have struggled to populate the world in the Middle Ages, when everyone had black teeth and seriously gippy breath. So the next time you are getting it on and you secretly congratulate yourself on selecting such a fragrant partner, think again! Their armpits could smell like a dog's nonsense . . . you simply would not know!

SUBTLE EMPATHY

As a Jedi relies on the force, so too must a couple rely on subtle empathy. Make sure you are always aware of anything on the radar that might cause your partner upset. It could be a sensitive subject, or a certain situation that triggers distress in which your partner will need you to know what they're thinking and that you are there for them. The most effective way to do this is a squeeze of the hand or even a unifying look, as anything more supportive might cause a 'critical mass' emotion-wise, affecting your partner's ability to cope. Sharing subtle empathy will improve all your partner's stresses no matter how small. Even if all they are doing is crying at *Kung Fu Panda* it's a good idea to be there for them.

SURPRISE HOLIDAYS

The gesture of startling your partner by suddenly informing them they are going abroad to somewhere seriously warm is not without its appeal. However, it is paramount that the holiday surpriser avoids one very common pitfall. This is the act of placing a packed suitcase by the door as a visual clue that the impromptu vacation is a firm and imminent reality.

In fact, all this will achieve is to cause the recipient to go 'OH MY GOD, THEY'RE KICKING ME OUT! WHAT HAVE I DONE?!', and be so stressed it will take an entire holiday or city break to get over.

TELLING YOUR PARTNER ABOUT YOUR DREAMS

Your partner is not really interested in your dreams as they are usually incoherent. The only time it is permissible to tell your partner about them is when you have one in which they cheat on you. Should this occur, common protocol is to refer to the real-life version of your partner as 'Complete Bastard!' for about twelve hours (forty-eight hours max).

TELLING YOUR PARTNER THEY DON'T LOOK GOOD

This is absolutely essential but should always be well timed. For instance, telling your partner they have failed to notice that their morning hair makes them look like a shallot, just as their cab pulls into the driveway, is an example of *bad* timing. Similarly, informing your other half that their shirt is so creased it looks like it's been bummed by a fox, just as the TV cameras start rolling, is *another* example of *bad* timing.

In general, any questions about your partner's appearance should be delivered by leaving enough of a timeframe to rectify whatever detail is wrong (e.g. change their shoes, reselect an entire outfit or iron their hair). If convenient, it is well worth playing some small part in your partner's outfit based on what level of fashion proficiency your partner has agreed you have obtained. Generally speaking you will usually be allowed to pick out your partner's shoes. Honesty should always be in play when it comes to matters of appearance, so remember not to ask questions like 'Do these shoulder-pads make me look like a quarterback?' if you do not want the answer.

THE 'D' WORD

In the same way you should never throw a hand grenade at someone unless you're certain you have a) pulled the pin, and b) identified the intended recipient, one must never threaten Divorce in an argument. Once the 'D' word has been uttered it is permanently on the table and a marriage can never then be properly 'unfragged'. It suddenly becomes a possibility and should never be given airtime – unless, of course, you have just discovered that your partner is no longer the original design.

Once you have become an item it may be tempting to inform your partner that you consider them to possess all the best composite parts of all your former partners. This is considered reckless behaviour (particularly if it is conveyed from man to woman) as it will land you in serious trouble (e.g. 'You've got arms just like my ex Judy had, skin like Penelope's, a smashing sense of humour not dissimilar to Claire's and a cracking pair of knockers like Val's').

The reason this usually ends in a tasering is that partners like to be considered as unique. They should be treated as though they have broken the mould and not described like a desperately unmarketable film, 'All the magic of *Harry Potter* with the despair of *Nil by Mouth* thrown in' etc. On falling for your partner, all aspects of them should be hereafter described as superior to any previous partners (e.g. 'Judy's arms were like those of a Victorian street fighter, you could light a match on Penelope's skin, Claire used to sulk through *Fawlty Towers* and Val's bum was bigger than Kent' and so on).

THE SHOUTY ROOM

Every household will have an area where most of the arguments take place. This is almost always the kitchen. Some believe the kitchen is the go-to shouty room because it is the place where things get heated up or because most people in there are hungry and irritated, but really it is because the kitchen is the most likely room where you'll just get under each other's feet. Anyone not wishing to engage in an argument should tread carefully when in and around the shouty room. Conversely, anyone wishing to have a tear-up over something (and indeed everything else that is bothering them about a person) should make a beeline for the shouty room and lurk in wait for their victim.

TIME APART

Being away from your partner for lengthy periods of time is a bit like the daytime 1990s quiz show, *Going for Gold*, in that it is good while also being dreadful. Solitude can be quite liberating, allowing one to choose one's own fun pursuits for the day. The trouble with this, however, is that these pursuits will suddenly seem less fun without your partner around. Don't rely on friends for company until you truly feel you're going mad. It is better to make the most of your time apart and try to enjoy this new dynamic for as long as you can. Once you are officially missing your partner you are permitted to persistently stay in touch with them. Call them, text them, Skype them on your tablet and take the tablet down to the pub.

The bar staff will usually be happy to provide you with a baby chair for your tablet, such that your partner can be propped up comfortably at the pub table and can enjoy the ambiance with you. During your intimate Skype pub evening it is important you do not offer your partner a drink from the pub, since Baileys is really hard to get out of an iPad.

WAKING YOUR PARTNER

There will be times when you may need to interrupt the lie-in of your loved one (e.g. lateness for pressing appointment or kitchen on fire). At the time of writing there is no known method for succeeding at this. What we *can* tell you, however, is a method that *doesn't* work – namely allowing a sausage dog into your partner's chamber while they are asleep naked above the covers. This is because, arguably, there is little more disturbing than to be hit in the midriff by a panting cylinder while still in a deep sleep.

WEDDING ANNIVERSARIES

These are a lot like monthly editions of those 'build your own Spitfire' magazines that start in January (the ones where the first one is 99p). You're really enthusiastic about the first and even show some interest in the next two or three, by which point you think: 'Sod this! I simply cannot be arsed.' And why should you be? You know you're both in love; why should you have to prove it? However, if you are at that 'first edition' stage of your married life and are mortified by the idea of forgetting your 'special day', slap the date in a silver picture frame and put it on the grand piano. Not only will this serve as a fool-proof memo, it will also double up as an aesthetically pleasing conversation piece all year round.

That said, we have marked some of the bigger occasions in our married life, and our tenth anniversary was our favourite by far. We invited our ten closest friends – not because it was the tenth but rather because the number of close friends we have is exactly ten! We had a lovely supper in the garden on a dining table we'd set up with black chandeliers and candles. After supper we thanked everyone for being there for us and opened a bottle of Krug.

Our wedding video had been filmed on a Super 8 in black and white and one of our friends played it for us set to 'The Beat Goes On' by Sonny and Cher, which was bloody fantastic.

WHEN YOUR PARTNER IS ILL

There will be times in your relationship when it is your turn to become the nurse, and we are not alluding to some costume-based role-play here (we took that back to the fancy dress shop ages ago). Of course illness can often be a very serious thing which requires a great deal of strength and commitment from everyone involved. For the purposes of this heading, however, we are referring to non-self-induced minor debilitating illnesses, such as coughs, colds, man flu (which is basically a cold) and general flu (which is basically general flu).

Usually one person in the relationship will be much better at being the 'nurse' and will generally get the short straw when it is their turn to be ill. Regardless as to whether you're Florence Nightingale or Florence Seriously-you-can't-be-that-ill-ingale, here are some guidelines to help make you a better carer:

ALLOW THE AM DRAM
The worst thing about a partner with a cold is that

they instantly start talking and acting like the burnt version of Ralph Fiennes in *The English Patient*. Sometimes they will even do a geriatric voice, despite not being geriatric. You have to allow them to do all of this, no matter how bad their acting seems to be. They are basically 'becoming' the cold in a bid to eventually beat it.

KEEP THEM COMPANY

If you have the reserves to do this, because being ill can be a lonely business at times, do try to spend time with them. And by 'spend time with them' we mean actually spend time next to them, not about ten metres away from them upwind. In fact, you should continue to be as intimate as you would be normally, because let's face it, that cold is in the post for you as well (see *What Nasty Bug Goes Around, Comes Around*).

PACE YOUR PATIENCE

Remember, it's a malady marathon not a sickie sprint. Always provide a level of care and compassion you can keep up consistently. Even if all you can manage is entering the room with a Michael Jackson sanitising mask to throw them paracetamol in the same way you throw bread for angry geese, this is better than rushing around for them for the first hour before snapping at them for taking the piss.

THROW MONEY AT IT

Buy every type of cough sweet, every brand of cold flu remedy, nasal sprays, vapour rub, everything. They will love that. To them it will be a form of retail sickie therapy.

WHAT NASTY BUG GOES AROUND, COMES AROUND

Unless you have a constitution of a rhino you are going to catch your partner's bug. Therefore it is essential that you care for them as well as you can since soon they will have to care for you. For this reason, really flag up everything you do for them so they will remember to do the same for you. 'I've put actual lemon in your Lemsip, look, and I've plumped up your pillow for you.' Similarly, if you are the first to fall ill, your level of neediness will be directly proportional to theirs when they succumb to your lurgy.

VASECTOMY

After a certain age, the male reproductive organs bear a lot of similarity to the Samurai warrior of ancient Japan: once roused they can be lethal, yet they often opt to fall on their sword as a mark of fealty. They are also both frequently referred to as 'Bushi' but that's another matter.

Relative to childbirth it is understood that the vasectomy is a painless procedure. The greatest consternation of undergoing such an operation is the unwritten rule that the nurse involved will be inextricably pretty. Should you find your genitals in close alignment with such a nurse it is important to relax, safe in the knowledge that within seconds a ginger-bearded doctor with teeth like a dead pirate will enter the room, acting as a sexual counterweight.

Manners, Misunderstandings and Social Mortifications:

How to Avoid Embarrassing Situations

Life in the twenty tweens or whatever we eventually decide to call this decade is a social minefield. People only had to worry about minding their p's and their q's in the olden days. Whereas now we've *the entire alphabet* of convivial pitfalls to contend with thanks to social media. Compared to us, the Victorians had it easy. I mean, sod worrying about how dark your tights need to be if you're grieving for Great Aunt Winnie. It's nothing compared to having a smartphone that hates you so much it turns your perfectly normal texts into the ramblings of a sex-crazed madman who's been kicked in the head by a horse. So here's all the help Steph and I can offer you on how to avoid and recover from finding yourself in any of the many forms of modern social duress.

– Dom

ADRENALINE

At some stage of your life you might have to take part in an event that creates a level of adrenaline; this may be a television appearance or a cake-judging competition which you only just made it in time for. In these instances it is fine to shake slightly, although if you do need to steady your hand, make sure it is your partner's elbow you are quivering up against and not some old lady you do not even know.

BAD GIFT RECEPTION

The skill of happily receiving a below-par present is something everyone living through modern peacetime should learn. Even if the product is so 'off the mark' you feel like smashing the place up, it is important to keep it together. Poor present reception is the only instance when briefly disengaging with honesty is permissible. On receipt of the sub-standard endowment it is paramount that nobody sees the glitch between your deep unhappiness and your projected joy. Similarly, any vocal pause will also give the game away. E.g. 'Oh . . . it's . . . some frog bookends . . . Great, because I really . . . really love . . . frog . . . bookends (*inner sigh*).'

Instead you should instantly rejoice over the gift, being sure to deflect attention from it via quick praise of the gift giver, such as: 'Oh my God, are they bookends? In frog form? Oh God, how beautiful, that was so clever of you. How brilliant of you to think of that.' Anyone anticipating a bout of extremely poor gift receiving may wish to arm themselves with a party popper. At the height of despair this can be discharged, creating a tiny flare of distraction.

BAD GRAMMAR

There is nothing worse in the world than the use of bad grammar. Many people share this view and take it upon themselves to correct people whenever their syntax is poor. These are referred to as Grammar Police. We, however, are the Grammar Nazis. If someone says, 'It will be determined by which door we walk through' we will goose-step over to them and say, 'It will be determined by the door *through which* we walk.' So remember to a) learn correct grammar, and b) enjoy the view from your high linguistical horse as you trot about correcting people.

We will now convey the same information for people with bad grammar:

There is nowt worse in the world than use of bad grammar. Plenty folk well think this and literally take it on them to put folk right whenever they talk wrong and that. These bad boys are grammar police but we are loads worse. If a bloke say 'I'll know when i go through door won't I', We say 'No mate . . . that's BANG OUT OF ORDER' 'You're meant for say 'I'll know when it's door THOUGH WHICH I've bin through'. So remember to D) talk proper A) look out for everyone thinking your a dick wen you tell um theyz gotz it wrong.

BOASTING

Nobody really cares if you have a new girlfriend, house, car, whatever, and they certainly don't want to be reminded of it every twenty seconds. If you do turn up in a burnt orange brand new Bentley and really want the world to think you have arrived, in all manner of speaking, make sure you own the bloody thing in the first place, as a rented one really doesn't cut it! The innuendo is really that hideous phrase (assume northern accent), 'I am considerably richer than yow!' You should never judge a man by his house or his car. Our other car is a Reliant Robin!

BORE FU

Bore Fu is the art of being able to combat disinterest in a conversation without damaging the esteem of the person doing the boring. The moment you find yourself in the headlock of a spiritless anecdote you should be ready to deploy some Bore Fu. Rapid energising questions must be fired back against the flow of the anecdote such that the teller is thrown off his or her guard and is no longer able to plough on as they would normally do. Any agitation caused towards the bore in the re-routing of their story should be countered by electric enthusiasm. After a period of confusion the bore will become exhilarated to be knocking their story out of the park, even though it is no longer quite their story. Like Tantric sex, Bore Fu should re-energise both parties involved. Here is an example of effective Bore Fu:

MAN: Are you a fan of cricket at all?
STEPH: It's not really something on my radar. Why?
MAN: I am. I'm a keen fan of cricket.

STEPH: Why do you love it?

MAN: You get to meet a lot of people through playing cricket. And the best thing about them is that the people who play cricket are usually the people who like cricket which is handy really, the other day I was just coming out to bat and—

STEPH (deploying Bore Fu): To bat, yes, in your cricket whites?

MAN: We wear white, yes, and I was just coming out to—

STEPH: Really, I always wondered how you cope with grass stains on the whites?

MAN: Wha-er. We just put them on a really hot wash . . . so I was just coming out to ba—

STEPH: Of course, you hot wash them! Silly of me. Is it a bio or non-bio for cricket whites?

MAN: A non-bio!

BORE FU (ADVANCED)

Here is another conversation trick to keep the other person on their toes. If the person you are talking to suddenly touches on a subject closer to your heart than the previous one, simply say, 'Oh, now suddenly you've become interesting.' This is not rude. Nobody minds about when they become interesting in a conversation. They will just be overjoyed to have become interesting in the first place.

DIVERT EMBARRASSMENT TOWARDS YOURSELF

The best way to overcome any embarrassing situation is to instantly magnify it by broadcasting it at the highest level. This will turn the incident into a celebration and people will think you are very funny as a bonus. For instance, if you turn up to a sixties theme party and suddenly realise the combination of your wafty blouse, feathers and thick black eyeliner have given you more of a buccaneer look than that of a bohemian flower child, simply stand proudly in the centre of the room where all can see you and confidently say, 'I look like bloody Jack Sparrow, don't I?'

FASHION *FAUX PAS* (ACCESSORIES)

Unsightly or unsettling accessories can easily be removed by the perpetrator, which means a much more confrontational approach can be employed. Any confusion or aggression you feel towards the offending article can be clarified through the use of a single profanity. For example, on meeting an alpha male golfer sporting a ridiculous sash round his head . . . stand and point saying, 'What's with the sodding headband?' Once the offender is subdued, remove yourself from the scene, using only peripheral vision to confirm when the article has been removed.

FOREIGN WORD OVER-PRONOUNCEMENT

Some people believe they will convey a level of international sophistication by enunciating foreign foods and names as they are pronounced in their country of origin; e.g. instead of pronouncing the pasta Rigatoni as 'Rigga-Toe-Knee' they will say 'Reega-toe-neeeeeeeee', often pulling a face like they are conducting an orchestra. There is an English phrase for this practice and the phrase is 'Very Wank'.

It is not ignorant to say Parmegiano instead of 'PaaaaaaamereJANO'. It is simply what it is called here. Similarly there is no need to cover people in a pint of phlegm whenever you say 'Pierre'. If you find you have a friend like this, pull them up on it but be careful not to inform them that what they are doing is indeed 'Very Wank' because they are most likely to retort with 'Actually, I think it is pronounced "Tres Wonk".'

FOREIGN WORD UNDER-PRONOUNCEMENT

While it is important not to be 'Very Wank' and insist foreign words must be over-pronounced, it is important to guard against being 'Not Wank Enough' in the under-pronouncement of them. Ideally, if you are speaking in a foreign language, it's then quite a good idea to have a stab at the accent.

STEPH: When I worked at NATO I had a colleague called Terry who spoke fluent French in a fluent Bolton dialect. He would go 'Bon-Joo-er. Germ appell Terry, common tally vu? Jer tra-vail dans leh Burrow day L'OTAN.' Nobody in Belgium knew what on earth he was talking about.

FORGETTING NAMES

Providing you don't click your fingers absently at the person whose name you have forgotten at precisely the point when you are saying their name, there is nothing wrong with forgetting someone else's name. Forgetting your own name is a different matter, however; if you are doing that, you need to slow down. If, though, you remain mortified at the prospect of forgetting a name – e.g. if you have to introduce them – an effective method is to say to them, 'I am so sorry, I have forgotten your name'. Then when they say 'Janet' you reply 'No, I know that, I meant your surname'. This throws a bit of a curve ball, allowing you to stealth-grab their name. Try and remember when you have used this ploy and on whom as this method only works once.

DOM: One of the worst instances of name forgetfulness was a guest who introduced his partner thus: 'This is my wife Annie. Oh God, no it's not; it's my girlfriend Sara!' Hugely embarrassing!

FRIENDLY RUDENESS

Subjecting someone you have only just met to a

constant level of friendly rudeness will put most people instantly at ease. Dispensing with politeness will prevent both of you from slipping into a boredom coma and will instead effectively fast-track your friendship. Friendly rudeness is very much a two-way street so, before embarking on it, it is important to check with yourself that you don't mind it being done to you. If the recipient of friendly rudeness begins placing his/her head firmly against your own, you have misjudged the level of friendly rudeness.

GREETING PEOPLE YOU'VE ALREADY MET

When meeting someone for the second time onwards it is imperative you greet them with a hug. A hug is a non-verbal way of expressing the words, 'If the building we are in begins to burn down I've totally got your back.' Even if this isn't true it will put the recipient at ease. You should note that since a hug is a warm greeting, it is only feasible in social circles and should never strictly be used for professional engagements, like returning to your bank manager for a loan. And certainly, when he says yes, don't ask him if you now have to have sex with him. Awkward silence will follow.

HIPSTER RETALIATION

Gentrified towns in Britain now generate a ready number of young men and women whose look is deemed cool by the cool. These people are hipsters. Encountering hipsters can be daunting, particularly since the menfolk consider it 'deck' to cultivate bushy beards. When travelling through the radius of a hipster community it is important to keep a small black carrier bag handy (the type you get from an off-licence when buying wine). On sighting the bearded menfolk, carefully place the handles of the carrier bag over either ear, being careful not to smother your mouth. In doing so, you will have created a 'bag beard', which will break the ice and cause hilarity among your friends and hipsters alike. A bag beard can be worn effectively by both male and female.

NOTE: While 'Deck' means 'cool' in hipster-speak, 'Ant' does not mean 'uncool'. 'Ant' in hipster-speak means 'Ant'.

HONESTY

This is widely considered 'the ketchup of all the virtues' because it improves anything it is used on. Deploying honesty in everything you think, say or do is not only advisable . . . it's the law. It is possible to be honest about almost anything provided this is followed up by being kind. In order to remember the order of these actions it is worth noting the adage 'Don't just get the turd on the table; get the turd on the table, then polish it.'

HOW NOT TO BE BORING

Almost all of us find our own lives fascinating. And why wouldn't we? We're the central character in our own daily film, even if that film is just about doing a bit of shopping and picking the kids up from school. The harsh reality is that most people won't be as interested in you as you are. They are too busy being the star of their own blockbuster film entitled *The Day I Washed the Car* or some such other banality. In short, there will be times when people find you boring just as you at times will find them 'a bit stuffy'. In order to keep other people's interest in you at a maximum here are some things to avoid:

1. Don't brag about property, possessions, or how much things cost.
2. Don't tell people how you travelled to the place you are at.

DOM: My sister and I have a great coping mechanism for dealing with people who spend an entire party talking about how they had arrived there. We question each other about our own journey even though we have probably travelled together: 'How did you get here?' 'I came here with you?!' 'Oh really, jolly good show.'

3. It is fine to talk about your children. They are important to you. Just do it in short bursts and try and sift for the most interesting things that have happened to them recently rather than a full presentation on how they got on in the paddling pool etc.

4. If your jaw is hurting or you feel a bit dizzy, you are talking too much. Imagine how everyone else feels.

5. Make sure most of your anecdotes don't involve you winning at something. People are much more interested in things you have severely messed up. If you are the hero all the time people will be bored.

6. If you sense you have banged on about yourself a little too long, then it is your duty to defuse this with a quip: 'But enough about me . . . what do *you* think about me?'

HOW TO DISAGREE IN PUBLIC

The archetypal model for a British (particularly English) person is one of Politeness and Repression. Indeed, bottling everything up might have worked in the Victorian age, most likely because there were a lot more horrible things that could happen to you, so if everyone had let it all out there would probably have been riots (but polite riots, where you would smash in Selfridges windows and allow any lady looters present to enter first).

Of course, nowadays politeness is still important, yet we no longer need repression in the same way we no longer need our appendix. We've moved on. The modern Brit, therefore, should be polite yet honest. If you fail to agree with someone, speak up, and then self-deprecate. For instance, if someone tells you they don't like Gyles Brandreth,* whereas you do (because he seriously is brilliant), then you reply: 'I love him, what a shame, I think he's brilliant, I must be a bit strange.' If it's something more serious, you should use the same approach but drop the self-deprecation: 'I don't necessarily agree with you; you've got some valid points there however.'

*Seriously, Gyles Brandreth is so brilliant. He spoke at a do we went to recently and blew our minds. We swear everything he said was hilarious and seemed to have been plucked from thin air. If there were any justice in the world, Gyles Brandreth would be king. There, we said it!

INDISCRETION

Being indiscreet is hugely harmful and easy to avoid. Secrets should not be used as currency to buy esteem from others. Even if the secret is eating a hole in you, let it. It will pass. Have faith in yourself to generate something else interesting to talk about.

INTERNET HISTORY

Going online is like leaving footprints in the snow, so if you've been anywhere suspect it's important to hit the 'delete history' button, which is the equivalent of a super-effective snow flattener for the purposes of this metaphor. The last thing you need is your partner discovering what you fantasise over and, in many cases, act on using your credit card. We are, of course, referring to internet clothes shopping,

where hiding your trail of purchases is essential if
you don't want to get yelled at in the kitchen.

*Why, what were *you* thinking of!?

KNOWING WHEN TO LEAVE A PARTY

All 'guide to life books' on the market will come
up short in one area or another. This book is
no exception. We have no idea when to leave a
party. There are some parties we are still at. You are
asking the wrong people. Move on.

MISJUDGING BOUNDARIES

When hosting guests it is often tempting to try and
accelerate the rapport by cutting to jocular vulgarity in
an attempt to set them at ease. While it is important to
push the envelope on a one-to-one basis (see *Friendly
Rudeness*), it is much more complicated to do so when
speaking to a group.

DOM: A friend of a friend of ours had a party once
and on our arrival their opening gambit to the
entire room was: 'Two things: if you're going to
have a sh*t, do it in the loo, and don't wipe your

c∗ck on the curtains.' Even for those with the most accommodating envelope-pushing apparatus, this would be considered too much. Of course this kind of bawdy vernacular might have better airtime later in the event and could even be rather amusing, but lewd conversation such as this must be earned. You must never start with it.

OBJECT RAGE

Punching a cupboard door after you have hit your head on it, or wildly stabbing a wind-buckled umbrella up and down into a litter bin, is a perfectly acceptable way to convey anger or frustration. In so doing you are downloading all of your aggression in one theatrically pleasing display. In some cases, however, the exhibition of object rage can betray a deeper level of frustration, like in the incident described below.

STEPH: My friend dropped some shopping once and proceeded to seriously bollock her boyfriend, Kevin, even though he was five miles away from the supermarket car park at the time: 'Oh, thanks a bastard lot, Kevin! Look what you've made me do now! The crackerbreads are all smashed thanks to you, Kevin!'

PEOPLE WHO MAKE STATEMENTS AS QUESTIONS

It is really annoying? To try and take in information? From someone who is constantly raising their inflection at the end of each statement? Leaving a sort of patronising gap just to see if they haven't left you behind with whatever they are prattling on about? This dreadful practice was originally started with antipodean backpackers but has now become much more widespread and so must be dealt with head-on. Whenever anyone speaks to you in this vernacular, the best thing to do is look puzzled and shake your head after each inflection.

POLITICS

Most people know that bringing politics to any group discussion will invariably end in tears. There is nobody on earth whose political affiliations won't cause offence to others. Don't think for a second that not bothering with politics will get you off the hook either! Not being interested in politics is still a political view and not a popular one! In fact it makes you the one faction all the other parties agree to hate. But what do you care? You're not even reading this entry, are you, because it gives POLITICS as the heading. Discussing politics requires everyone to know every political party's manifesto.

Rarely, however, does anyone do this, preferring instead to rant on about their firm but poorly researched beliefs in the vain hope that they can convert others (see *How Not to be Boring*). In truth, your political views (or lack of them) will be determined only by a) what your parents vote, b) socioeconomic status, c) level of working environment, and d) the press. Once these factors have determined your views, you will argue them forever and nobody will listen to them. Because, really, modern politics is just a popularity contest with mostly unpopular candidates.

DOM'S WORLD-CHANGING POLITICS IDEA: I think they should create an independent board that judges every policy of whoever is in power. A bit like they do with the dances on *Strictly*. E.g.: 'Wow, your education policy was so inclusive and progressive. You're really growing into this competition, it's an Eight from me!' The best policies will then go through to the *Britain's Got Policies* grand final . . . I mean, obviously the idea needs a bit of fine-tuning but it all makes perfect sense!

POOR CUSTOMER SERVICE

If you are ever in a shop or restaurant in the British Isles, you'll be experiencing poor customer service unless you are in a seventeen-roomed guest house deep in the garden of England (ahem). When poor service occurs it may be tempting to sub-vocally vent to a partner up to the return/arrival of the waiter/assistant/bank manager who is currently ruining your day, whereupon your rage will most likely shrink like spinach in a hot pan. This is inadvisable, as not only will the poor service continue, but you will also suffer internal damage, effectively allowing the disconsolate clerk to affect your lifespan. The phrase 'Excuse me . . . you're clearly having a bad day but how can I make it better?' is clinically effective in all instances.

QUEUING

British people seem to be born with the misconception that as a race they are good at queuing, even though every individual Brit is 'really quite seriously shit at it'. Having some level of queueing experience (e.g. being in a queue) does not mean you are good at queuing. In the same way that being caught in a tornado does not make you good at winds. If you have done any of the following, then you most likely have a poor queue gene: a) tutting at people in front of you in the queue, b) phone gazing when the queue is moving forward, c) not instantly heading to 'cashier number six please' when you have been asked to, d) glaring at queue breakers, e) squaring up to a queue breaker, or f) taking a ticket and leaving the queue scene, then missing when your ticket is called.

FACT: Germany is actually one of the best races at queuing because they tend to be much more relaxed about the process and often let people go in front of them. Go figure!

RECEIVING CATERING COMPLAINTS

Should you work in the catering or hospitality industry, you will from time to time receive complaints. Some of the complaints will be genuine, whereas others will merely be clients 'trying it on'. It is important you do *not* try to identify which one of the above this is. Digging in your heels and failing to be courteous will only increase the volume and range of the remonstration as well as risking the complainer 'going batshit'.

In most instances you should offer to entirely replace the meal in question. If, for example, a client rightly or wrongly complains of an overcooked steak, bring them the entire meal again and be sure to provide free interim beverages for him/her and any of their party while the matter is dealt with. Should the client fail to be sated by your attempt to put the matter right, simply inform them there is no charge whatsoever for the meal. Your generosity will work as a rudimentary honesty box, ensuring they guiltily spend double the price of the meal in your bar. Almost all restaurants in the world, please take note!

SOCIAL MEDIA NO-NOS

FAKING LOLS

This is worse than faking an orgasm in our opinion. Why would you pretend you laughed at something that you didn't find remotely funny?

FOOD PHOTOS

Why would you think anyone would want to see a photo of something prior to you digesting it? Okay, it's moderately preferable to you taking a picture at the other end of proceedings, but only just. The only exception is when preparing menus.

KISSES

It isn't a good idea to worry about whether or not to end an email, text or direct message with an X at the end of it, or two smaller xx's as fashion currently dictates. Either don't do kisses at all, or do them for everyone. Men should not worry that other men will judge them just because they do a little kiss at the end. If the whole cyber-kisses thing isn't your scene you can always go your own way. We like to end many of our texts to people with 'KR' but are considering retiring this, as many people think they have just received a text from Keanu Reeves.

LASHING OUT

One great thing about writing angry letters to soon-to-be ex-friends, ex-boyfriends or ex-girlfriends was that letters had a cool-off period. You could get it all out then send it in the morning if you wanted to (and you never wanted to). Nowadays you have the ability to make a total knob of yourself by showing how short a fuse you have by lashing out immediatley online.

NOT THE FACEBOOK

Facebook is the social media equivalent to a massive dinner party with everyone shouting at once. If you bellow loud enough you might reach the people you are trying to impress but you will irritate everyone else. There are thousands of ways to mess up on Facebook, but below are what one half of us believe to be the big hitters. Or big shitters if that's nicer.

GOOGLING IT!: We've all seen these posts: 'Hi guys, does anyone know a good plumber in the area?' Oh,

sorry, now you want me to be your private search
engine, do you? Lazy gits!

PICTURES OF FEET BY A POOL OR A BEACH: Yeah,
we get it, you're on holiday, but it's Facebook not
Gloatbook, you do realise? Plus your feet are ugly! And
the reason your feet ming is because they are feet.

POSTING ABOUT YOUR BABY: Here's the thing. Your
children are beautiful and fascinating to you. That's
what makes them your children. They're just not
that fascinating to the rest of cyberspace. Keep your
pictures in a family album; they are private – don't post
them to the universe; it's pissing the universe off. And
don't think any witty comments about the photo are
going to save you. A photo of a toddler on a tricycle
with 'Eat your heart out Bradley Wiggins' is again only
great where it belongs: in *your* photo album at home.

REQUESTING HELP WITH YOUR GAME: We don't care
how many times you ask. We are NOT going to help
you with your pretend-cows on your pretend-farm.
Nor am I going to help you crush more candies, kill
more zombies, or waste any more of your own time.

TWAT

The title for this heading is the name we like to give Twitter. This is because it is shorter and more fun to say than bloody Twitter. More and more people we meet are doing this, so we would be entirely grateful if you would do the same. Twat is like a more upmarket soirée than Facebook, so you need to up your game or risk everyone turning themselves away from you. There isn't a lot that irritates us on Twat but, for what it's worth, here is a list of the worst things:

THINGS THAT ANNOY US ABOUT TWAT

Charity spamming
Hashtag abuse
Alan Sugar

THE 'C' WORD

The rudest of swear words, the one beginning with C is one you should reserve for special occasions. In fact, it should only be released under the following circumstances: a) describing someone utterly despicable, and b) describing a situation that is utterly despicable. Otherwise it should be kept cooped up in your swear hive, like the queen bee (or queen C if that's nicer). And use your 'F' word drones to do most of your work for you.

THEATRICAL FLATULENCE

The only thing in the world funnier than flatulence is flatulence accompanied by some degree of theatricality. This can take the form of a well-rehearsed narrative such as 'Listen to this, it's not to be missed: it's Britain's number one.' Even more pleasing to an audience, however, is the introduction of a kind of physical slapstick to the act of breaking wind. For instance, teetering back on a chair while reading a newspaper, then letting a light fart provide the momentum to send you crashing backwards, is amusing. Even better than this, however, is the 'trump hug'. Namely a well-timed low baritone guff deployed at the moment you hug a loved one. This is not only theatrically pleasing but also indicates the offence emitted from them on receiving your embrace.

TIPPING

Be as generous as you feel is right or indeed you can afford but, in general, 10 per cent of the bill will probably just about get you into 'Service industry heaven' once you die, provided you tip the angels at the gates. The tip is bigger in America, of course, but then again so are the waiters.

NOTE: Be aware that overtipping can sometimes backfire horrifically. On our honeymoon, we'd finished an exhausting journey right across the globe at glacial speed, like the dot on the maps in the Indiana Jones films. We'd got to the hotel exhausted and one of the hotel staff, a little chap, came to help us with our cases. We gave him a hundred dollars and said 'This is for you. If you look after us . . . we'll look after you.' He thanked us and bowed nobly. We never saw him again. Lord knows where he went but we like to think he rushed home and told his family to pack their stuff and just buggered off.

UNISEX LOOS

Popularised by 1990s legal comedy drama *Ally McBeal* but a living hell in real life. Avoid.

WET PENNY

There is little more embarrassing than returning from the loo in a bar or restaurant with a patch of liquid on the crotch (usually in the shape of the landlocked African country, Chad). This is known colloquially as a 'wet penny' and should be dealt with quickly and professionally. The correct coping mechanisms vary depending on gender.

A male discovering a wet penny should immediately tip the nearest beverage over the offending area and shout 'Bloody hell, aren't I the clumsy one, I've thrown a whole pint down my c*ck!' Women on the other hand are advised to 'pack their pants in', a swift operation that involves the thighs imbibing any clothing around the crotch. At present no technology exists to help cope with this urine-based quandary, although some strong moves have been made to take this forward (see *Drunken Dragons' Den*). Blaming the patch on having been shat on by a bird is good, but hard to swallow.

Kicking about the Castle:
How to Make the Most Out of Your Downtime

Since Dom and I have been married we've never known what's going to happen next. Like crap chess players we're only ever one move ahead of the game. In the past when we did get a bit of downtime we were so blown away with it that we wasted a bit of it discussing what to do with it, which is ridiculous! We used to end up lounging on the sofa and watching TV, but that was before our job involved us, well, lounging on the sofa and watching TV . . . so things are more complicated now. Over the years, however, we've learnt to fast-track our relaxation and take it where we can. You can do the same, provided you put to memory the entire contents of this chapter. Or else have it laminated and carry it around with you. Or have it as a tattoo.

– *Steph*

ALWAYS HAVE SOMETHING COMING IN THE POST

In this day and age it is possible to order almost anything on the internet safe in the knowledge that it will usually arrive in the next few days. Having something delivered to your home that is neither a bill nor mass-produced sales drivel makes receiving the post fun. However, once you have experienced the thrill of receiving something that wouldn't fit through the letter box, there is a tendency to find it massively addictive.

This addiction must be sated such that there is always at least one thing arriving in the post for you on any given day. An added bonus to this approach is watching your postman become fitter on a day-to-day basis as he carries your heavy gifts to your door, like a boxer in a really slow training montage. It is often worth getting up to sign for your deliveries, especially if you are not a real fan of the dawn (see *Morning People*). This is because when receiving packages while half-asleep it is impossible to remember what you have ordered. This gives the self-gift the mystery of a real gift that someone else has bestowed on you.

ART GALLERIES

While visiting these institutions is never a guarantee of a good time, they can often be inspiring and interesting as long as you have some degree of knowledge or interest. One thing a visit to a gallery will guarantee, however, is the generation of a high volume of personal wind the moment you set foot in there (this is also the same with bookshops).

Having gallery wind is more often than not a joyous distraction, largely because the building you are in is usually very tall and airy, allowing you to enjoy your personal turbulence with little fear of repercussion. Do remember, however, if you are experiencing gallery wind while wearing headphones for a recorded tour, that everyone else is *also* wearing headphones . . . remove yours before taking the decision to fire one off.

BATHROOM

Never get a Jacuzzi bath. It will go wrong.
Never get a Jacuzzi bath. It will go wrong.
Never get a Jacuzzi bath. It will go wrong.
Never get a Jacuzzi bath. It will go wrong.
Never get a Jacuzzi bath. It will go wrong.
Never get a Jacuzzi bath. It will go wrong.

BEVERAGE NEMESIS

This is any alcoholic drink which has turned on you as a result of consuming way too much of it in a single session. One sip or even sniff of it will cause you to immediately barf up. Beverage nemeses have a half-life of eighty years, which means most of us must avoid them forever, so it is important to never overdo a drink you currently favour. Attempting to dilute a beverage nemesis will not only still induce a vom-athon but may also cause the mixer that you used to turn against you as well, acting as the beverage nemesis's sidekick. Popular beverage nemeses are Tequila shots, Sambuca, or any whiskey.

CARS

Cars should be solid and reliable but by no means do they have to be new. A Jaguar, for example, will see you through the reign of roughly three popes. If you have more cars than people in the family who need cars then you have too many cars. There is no good reason to own a fleet of vehicles, unless you want people to think you are a knobhead possessing a carbon footprint of a yeti with fluid retention.

CLEANERS

Having a cleaner is not only essential but also cost-effective. For the price of the cleaner you will receive a) a cleaner, and b) an inflated feeling of success within yourself because you are hiring a cleaner. Householders with a penchant for OCD may entertain 'cleaning for the cleaner' prior to their arrival. This is to be considered as ridiculous as assembling a lasagne prior to the arrival of a personal chef.

COMEDY RESTAURANT PEPPER REJECTION

An effective way of breaking up the joyless ceremony of being waited on (particularly in an Italian restaurant) is to wait until the moment the waiter returns to the table with the iconic pepper mill asking if indeed you would like some pepper on your food. Try to be mid-conversation at this point and, on hearing the question, give a vague 'yes' signal. Don't do anything too signposted, just the slightest of nods as if you were bidding subtly on something from the back of an auction house. The waiter will then proceed to grind pepper onto your food. At this point you must recoil in horror and shout at the top of your voice, 'NOT PEPPER!'

The look on the waiter's face will be worth it every time, and once your table erupts into laughter, he or she will also enjoy the joke (to a lesser extent than your table). Comedy restaurant pepper rejection is most effective against waiters who are new to the phenomenon, and over-familiarity with it may breed contempt.

DANCING

We can state from experience, having spent four days learning a rudimentary jive (to Dean Martin's 'That's Amore') on our wedding day, that the best type of dancing is the unrehearsed type. The adage 'Dance like nobody is watching' may seem like quite sage advice but it is only partially true. In fact, you should dance like nobody is watching your body but everyone is watching your face, because people (particularly British people) do have a habit of looking rather aggressive once they are 'in the zone'. Even the most fun dance moves can be spoilt slightly if the dancer is wearing an expression like Andy Murray having just stepped on a block of Lego. You may think you are looking cool and carefree taking part in YMCA, for example, but what you are really saying is: 'Y-M-C-A, YOU BASTARD!, Y-M-C-A, YOU BASTARD!' Any males should be aware that their dancing years are roughly the same years as a professional footballer is able to play for (aged between seventeen and forty). Of course there are other types of dance you are able to perform after this period.

DANCING A DRINK ON

A fun and upbeat way to prepare a drink for the evening is to gambol about vigorously to whatever is on your iTunes at the time. Dancing a drink on is especially effective if preparing a cocktail, as your gyrations will be congruent with the motion required to mix it. As well as this, your impromptu dance will get you in the mood for the drink you are about to self-gift. Another advantage is that by throwing shapes while putting your tipple together you are creating a talking point for any nervous guests that might be in the room at the time. Dancing your drink on is also a much more effective way of burning the extra twelve calories found in non-slimline mixers (see *Slimline Mixers*).

DRINK THIN

If you are trying to slim down and do not wish to compromise your inner party animal, the best option is to stay on spirits. These are best taken with water or ice to ensure your drink lasts longer. If your drink requires a mixer, use the full-fat version only (see *Slimline Mixers*). Even more important than this is to get excited about being out. Excitement curbs appetite. Fact.

FINE-TUNING YOUR MEAL

Nobody will have a problem with your wish to change or upgrade an aspect of your lunch. You will incur no extra cost in doing so PROVIDED your request is reasonable and carried out politely. For example, 'Excuse me, would it be all right to get a little more cheddar in my ploughman's because I really do love cheddar, you see?' is a perfectly permissible request, whereas 'Not enough fooking cheddar on there for me!' is not.

DRAWING ROOM

Whether it be your lounge, drawing room, salon, sitting room or chill outage, the drawing room is important, as it is where you will do the majority of your relaxing. This room should be designed with relaxation in mind. There is no obligation to have anything you don't want in there other than possibly a sofa to sit on. You will also need side tables to rest drinks on as well as a cabinet for the drinks. But other than that there is no obligation to have anything else. Apart from a television, of course. Without a television you'd be cut off from the world and wouldn't be aware of great personalities who enrich reality TV shows etc. Aside from a sofa, side tables, a drinks cabinet and television, however, you are not obliged to have anything else in this very important room.*

*Other than nice lighting, ornaments, photographs, rugs, a grand piano, books, scatter cushions, fireplace, ornaments, a sound system, seven remote controls and a throwy thing for the dog.

GLASS DROPS

Upon hearing a bartender erratically smash a stack of pint pots in a pub, common procedure is to observe a three-second cheer. A much better way to react on hearing the report, however, is to pretend to be really angry about it. There are a great many hidden hilarities in life and subjecting a glass dropper to a massive mock bollocking from the other side of a pub is one of them.

HUNTING

In our spare time, both of us enjoy hunting in our own different ways. One of us has a penchant for shooting whereas the other does their hunting in the form of retail therapy. Both are very different sports yet, surprisingly, have very many similarities. So before you decide whether hunting Upland Game Birds or Massive Bargains is for you, here is some vital information on the code of hunting, along with its shopping equivalent.

GAME SHOOTING

A largely expensive pastime that has been practised for many centuries and in some areas is a part of British rural culture.

SHOPPING equivalent: Exactly the same as 'shooting' summary (replacing 'rural' with 'urban').

DRIVEN SHOOT

This is like a rough shoot but a lot less effort. The birds are driven at you by beaters and it's much, much more expensive.

SHOPPING equivalent: The internet. It's like going to Bicester Village in Oxfordshire but a lot less effort. The bargains are driven at you by aggressive marketing web sales strategists. Ends up being much more expensive.

HANGING BIRDS

This is the practice of hanging any game you have brought home by its neck for a period of time (a longer period of time will produce a richer taste). It is then prepared for the oven.

SHOPPING equivalent: Hanging clothes. This is the practice of hanging any garment the shopper has brought home on clothes hangers for a period of time (a longer period of time will produce a poor fashion taste). It is then prepared for eBay.

HUNTING SEASON

In the UK the game-hunting season starts on 12th August, known as the 'Glorious 12th' with grouse on the menu, and ends 1st February of the following year. Various bird seasons such as the black grouse come up and end in between.

However, outside of the UK it is possible to hunt all year round.

SHOPPING equivalent: Fashion seasons. Where once there were just two fashion seasons (spring/summer and autumn/winter) all that has recently changed, with the fashion season churning out fifty-two micro-seasons per year, making it possible to buy as many garments as possible as quickly as possible all year round.

LINE OF NINE

This is usually the number of shooters or 'guns' in a driven shoot; you will draw your number from a lot and stand in a line in that position, firing upwards at any game that flies overhead. The number you hold will go up by either one or three during each new drive.

SHOPPING equivalent: The Argos queue. Shoppers draw their ticket number from a till receipt and stand in a line in that position, firing furious glances upwards at the order screen. The number you hold will come up in either one hour or three seconds, depending on whether you stay or briefly vacate the store, respectively.

LOADER

A person who loads your gun ready for each shot. It is not uncommon to have two guns, with the loader readying one while you are using the other.

SHOPPING equivalent: High earner. This is a person who loads your credit card ready for each shop. It is not uncommon to have two credit cards, with the high earner readying one while you max out the other.

HEAD GAME KEEPER

The person responsible for making sure the birds fly in the right direction. They are usually tipped for their troubles.

SHOPPING equivalent: Floor staff. Store Managers' aides who refold all the blouses and dresses that you and everyone else has scattered all over the store. They are usually paid a minimum hourly wage for their troubles.

QUICK SHOT

An effective method of deploying the shot gun quickly and instinctively rather than taking time to firm up your aim. Most commonly used with grouse and partridge, as they appear much quicker than other game birds.

SHOPPING equivalent: Quick click. An ineffective method of quickly clicking your mouse on 'Complete sale' instinctively rather than taking time to weigh up the consequences. Most common in the January Sales as the bargains move much quicker than at other times of the year.

ROUGH SHOOT

This involves a group of guns who walk through an area, usually on private property. There is lots of walking about until a bird gets up in the air; then you have a pop at it.

SHOPPING equivalent: Going to Bicester Village: this involves lots of walking through a retail outlet and tackling a bargain before your nemesis (other shoppers) gets near it. If a bird tries to grab it off you during a frantic sale, you have a pop at her.

SHOOTING ATTIRE

For a driven shoot, guns wear plus-fours, stockings, wellingtons or stout hiking boots, a dull-coloured sporting coat down to the hips with large pockets, and a shirt and tie. A rough shoot is a little more relaxed.

SHOPPING equivalent: Shopping attire. For a Bicester Village visit, shoppers must wear something suitably chic, but flats are a must. Repeat, heels are for the novice shopper. Avoid heels at all costs. Internet shoppers should wear a dressing gown with an optional big 'f**k-off' towel on their head.

SHOOTING LUNCHES

A much anticipated group repast where morale will generally be high. Participants drink moderately so as not to cause shooting accidents later, but eat to excess.
SHOPPING equivalent: Shopping lunches. This is a much-anticipated one-on-one repast where morale will generally be judged on how slim the shopper's friend is in comparison to themselves. Participants eat the same or lower number of calories as their friend does and drink to excess.

WIPING THEIR EYE

This is the act of shooting a fellow hunter's bird once you are certain he or she has missed it. This is completely acceptable.
SHOPPING equivalent: Dress copying. This is the act of buying the same garment as a girlfriend once you are certain it is a hit. This is completely unacceptable (even if you buy it in a different colour).

IRISH COFFEE QUIZ

Irish coffee is without doubt one of the best things to make in your downtime. Just because; take our quick quiz to see if you are prepared to make one with as much dedication as we put in. Go on, it's not like you've got anything better to do, is it?

1. Do either you or your guests fancy an Irish coffee? y3, n2
2. Proceed with less complicated drinks for a while longer.
3. Do you have a tall deep glass that can accommodate Irish coffee? y6, n4
4. Do you have wine glasses? y5, n2
5. Are you prepared to look a 'bit of a knob'? y6, n2
6. Do you have brown sugar lumps (or dark granulated sugar)? y9, n2
7. Did the last requirement on that list sound even mildly erotic to you? y8, n9
8. Get a room.
9. Put sugar in the bottom of an empty clean glass.

10. Add Jameson's Whiskey (25 cl*).

11. Do you want to actually taste the whiskey in your Irish coffee?* y10, n12 (*50 cl recommended).

12. Add a strong amount of coffee in each of the glasses, approximately halfway up the glass.

13. Add hot water so the glass is now three-quarters full.

14. Using a rapid wrist action, stir to make sure the sugar is dissolved. Start slowly then proceed to beat off vigorously.

15. Did the glass shatter? y1, n17

16. Up your technique.

17. Aerate the double cream with a fork.

18. Has the cream gone all over the place? y20, n19

19. Liar.

20. It always does. Deal with it.

21. Continue to aerate the cream until it is just slightly thick.

22. Using the back of a spoon, slowly drizzle the cream to the desired level onto the surface of the contents.

23. Did the entire drink go beiger than an airport neck pillow instantly? y16, n24

24. Does the drink have varying stripes of dark brown to light brown (like a 1970s wallpaper)? y26, n29

25. Is the drink for yourself? y28, n27

26. Are you the type of person to deal with guests discussing your cavalier attitude towards cream dispensation behind your back? y28, n28

27. Serve and relax (but practise that pour).

28. Is the drink pretty much all black with a perfect white top (like a pint of Guinness or an Irish coffee, say)? y30, n26

29. Well done. You have won at IRISH COFFEE.

KIDS IN PUBS

Readers of a certain age (let's just say anyone who remembers pound notes) will most likely recall lengthy periods of their childhood that involved sitting in their parents' car in a pub car park with a bottle of Coke and a bag of crisps while their parents enjoyed the luxury of being inside the pub. Over the course of the evening, parents would return to the car as restless sparrows will to a nest, where they would replenish the refreshments of their young, before heading back inside. This was an effective way of enjoying an evening out while not having to pay a babysitter and, aside from the occasional bad look from a landlord when an inebriated parent accidentally asked for 'a *bottle* of crisps and a *bag* of Coke', it was a largely fool-proof method.

In today's times, however, parents would no more leave their children in a car than they would fail to furnish them with smartphones and tracker devices. This, along with the loosening of licensing laws, has determined that nowadays you're going to have kids in pubs. Many people witnessing a family with an infant in a pub will sub-vocalise scorn, muttering phrases like, 'You shouldn't have kids if you want to go to the pub.' It is important to remember that everyone has the right to a social and family life and, provided the children are well behaved, they should be made to feel welcome by everyone. Families who have lost control of their kids, however, can f*ck right off.

KINDLES

Kindles are the brown bag of the world of literature. They allow the user to consume erotic novels in public (if they want to) without anyone having the faintest idea. This, you might argue, gives them the edge in the books versus Kindles row. Then again, the joy of curling up with a good book and feeling its pages in your hands is something to factor in. In truth though, you don't have to *ever* pick a lane. You can, if you're up for it, enjoy both books and Kindles and nobody will think you are spineless (like a Kindle, not a book) just because you can't decide.

NOTE: Remember, if someone buys you a Kindle as a gift and you already have one, you can't fake joy using the line 'Oh well, you can never have too many Kindles.'

LUNCH

This is widely regarded as the most important meal of the day. A lunch, if carried out effectively, will furnish you with enough calories for the rest of the day. The metabolism will then become accustomed to dealing with one large sudden repast, leaving more time for it to 'chill'.

LONG ISLAND ICED TEA

This is the superhero of alcoholic beverages. Long Island Iced Tea is strong, multi-faceted and a master of disguise; one or two of these and you will believe a man can fly. This stalwart drink gets the iced tea part of its name because it actually resembles iced tea in colour, making it an extremely valuable ally at garden parties policed by teetotal grannies. It is also an extremely good honeymoon drink so if you're on honeymoon reading this, get to the nearest beach bar and get involved! Of course, you can also make this drink at home relatively easily, provided you don't mind making a massive load of mess when you drop the cocktail shaker all over the shouty room floor. Enjoy!

INGREDIENTS (serves 2)

1 shot Tequila (any decent)

1 shot white rum (any decent)

1 shot triple sec (any decent)

1 shot vodka (any)

1 shot gin (Gordon's)

1½ shots lime juice

2 shots sugar syrup

Crushed ice

Cola

2 highball glasses

A cocktail shaker

Lime slices

METHOD: Add the shots to the cocktail shaker along with the lime juice.

Ensure the cocktail shaker is closed unless the cleaner is coming that day.

Shake vigorously (see *Dancing a Drink On*).

Place the crushed ice into the highball glasses.

Ensure the cocktail shaker is now open.

Distribute the contents of the cocktail shaker evenly into the highball glasses.

Garnish with lime slices.

Serve and enjoy!

NOTE: It is not wise to mix loads of Long Island Iced Tea and store it carelessly in a cupboard as, horribly, inevitably, someone will mistake it for a single white spirit and will most likely think they have become a lightweight overnight for not being able to handle a G&T.

LOSING WEIGHT OR LOSING LOOKS?

Before deciding to lose weight it is important to confirm you are not one of those people who looks like a week-old party balloon once they have shed a few stone, e.g. Lenny Henry, Perez Hilton, Peter Jackson. If you're not one of those people who look hotter when a bit filled out then you may proceed with a sensible weight-loss programme. If you do look better as a beef tomato then just relax in your own beautiful skin. This is not an excuse to become any bigger, however. Remember, you don't see too many old fat people.

LUNCHEON ROULETTE

When ordering lunch it is not uncommon to struggle to decide between two dishes from the available fare. For example, 'a ploughman's' or a 'burger' may easily provide an arena of conflict. In almost all cases like this, one will be 'atrocious' and the other will be 'bloody yum'. This is known as Luncheon Roulette.

Just like the Roulette wheel at the casino, your chances of ordering the winner are roughly fifty-fifty (with the green zero being the chance of food poisoning). Asking a waiter which to go for is like asking a croupier which colour to bet on. Nobody knows how it will come out! Not even the chef. So the order must be placed and the best must be hoped for. While playing Luncheon Roulette, it is permissible to instantly and vocally regret your order, e.g. order the ploughman's and spend the entire time it takes to arrive repeating 'Should have got the burger. Should have got the burger.'

MATCH WINE WITH MOOD

The adage that reds are only to be taken with red meat and that white wines are only really palatable with fish, seafood and chicken etc. is mere superstition and is to be completely ignored. Some people will of course argue to the contrary and even go as far as to drink only certain reds with certain red meats, for example. These people are wine racists and should be shunned. Your criteria for selection of wine should be based on which wine you feel like drinking at that moment.

In the same way that walking against the direction of the floor arrows in Ikea will not cause the earth to spin backwards on its axis, drinking a Frascati with a Porterhouse steak will not cause the restaurant you are in to explode. As a quick and easy reference, here are some basic moods with their recommended wines.

MOOD

Tired — White

Thirsty — White

Not tired — Red

Not thirsty — Red

Overheated — White

Not overheated — Red

Tired, overheated, thirsty but not wanting White — Red

Not tired, thirsty, overheated but not wanting Red — White

Wanting Red — Red

Wanting White — White

Wanting Red when your partner wants White — Rosé

MCDONALD'S

As long as there are still days when people need to smash their face into a Big Mac (or a chicken burger if you're feeling healthy) there will always be McDonald's, get over it.

MUSEUMS

Like art galleries these can be hit or miss but it is important to be wary of the influence of statues. For example, if you visit the museum as a boy you may become aware of the irregularity of any alabaster testicles the statues of men may be equipped with. This is very useful information particularly if you have recently been worrying that your own testicles are not even and have quietly been trying to rectify the problem by regularly pulling at one of your own stones in the hope that your downstairs area will eventually even up. Statues' testicles will let you relax into the fact that it is normal to have one up, one down, like a lava lamp.

NOTHING DAYS

Arguably THE most important days of the year, nothing days are those in which you by choice pursue nothing whatsoever. Factoring in a nothing day is easily the quickest and most effective way to recharge your batteries. Rest-wise, a single nothing day is as effective as an entire weekend dicking about the house doing a couple of light jobs like putting up a picture or removing a mug. The following activities are permissible on a nothing day: a) sleep, b) bathroom visitation, c) having a sausage in a bun, and d) some time on the internet.

PINK

Rosé wine, the champion of compromise to couples at loggerheads over red or white everywhere.

PLANNING AN EVENING IN

There should be no planning for an evening in. Any planning time is better used as jumping-up-and-downtime in rejoicing over the fact that you are about to have an evening in. Once your jumping-up-and-downtime has ended, you and anyone else having the evening in should then move as quickly as you can to the area of your house where your most comfortable clothes are kept (see *Power-Walk Racing*). Dress in whatever you are most comfortable in. Wear a kaftan if need be, or a pair of pyjamas with a really baggy fly. There should also be a mild degree of food anticipation. Baked potatoes, omelettes, sausage on a scotch roll, or any other comfort food that causes you to do a dance and rub your hands together in glee. Remember, this is a real celebration so if you have access to balloons then now is the time to get them inflated. You will then need to select a suitable quiet night-in film. This should be chosen on the basis of how easy it is to fall asleep to, e.g. anything by David Lynch.

NOTE: Do not select *Braveheart* as your film to sleep to. You will constantly be ripped out of your sofa sleep, only to see blue faces roaring and charging at you.

PORN NAMES

Lounging about on a sofa while shooting the breeze with your partner will inevitably throw up the challenge of you both deciding on the stage names you would go by if you worked as a performer in the adult industry. This brief distraction has been around for over a decade but is still amusing in the same way Crazy Frog isn't. To create your porn name you will need:

- A memory strong enough to recall the name of your first pet.
- Knowledge of your mother's maiden name.

The former will become your first name and the latter will be the surname under which you will ply your hypothetical X-rated trade. Extra kudos will be given for having an epithet that sounds more like a rap star than anything remotely seedy (Steph Parker = Goldie Lyon). And extra, extra kudos will be provided for having a brand that makes it sound as though you cater for a very specific area of the adult industry (Dom Parker = Sophie Heathcote-Hacker).

NOTE: A useful offshoot of this distraction is to obtain the porn name of older members of your family, publicans and local politicians without them really knowing what is going on. This is known as 'Stealth porn naming' and will garner you an interim nickname for that person before a more suitable one comes about (see *Nicknames*).

POWER-WALK RACING
A hilarious way to keep fit while spending time around the home with your loved ones, power walking – the act of trying to beat your partner to whatever location in the house you are both headed for by walking more speedily than they are – is particularly good as a domestic competitive sport because everyone is usually as good and bad at it as each other. Nevertheless, the act of overtaking your partner in a particularly narrow bit of corridor is extremely satisfying.

PRIVATE NUMBER PLATES
As distasteful and unfashionable as a pony-tail on a man. These can also alert people who know you to the fact that you are somewhere you shouldn't be! Avoid.

SLIMLINE MIXERS
Calorie austerity in traditional mixer drinks is madness. In a bid to save twelve calories you are effectively weeing into the eyes of your ancestors. Moreover, the slimline version of the mixer will stop

the drink tasting nice and many brands are bad for you. When it comes to something like a gin and tonic you are either all-in or all-out.

TELEVISION

Over the last decade or so, televisions have shed a lot of weight and gained a great deal of confidence. With their massive behinds a thing of the past, it is possible to have a television in your room as big as the diagonal length of your door frame. This surge in screen size has prompted protest from many, who for some reason deem it vulgar to have a 'big f*ck-off TV'. Ignore these people entirely and have a television as big as you want and can afford. Never, however, mount a flat-screen TV on the wall, particularly over a fireplace.* Doing so is impractical, as straining your neck upwards is not the way to watch television. Television is a more intimate experience when you are gazing downwards slightly at it. Sticking one on the wall will also make your room look extremely ugly, especially when the TV is off.

*Unless you have one of those televisions that turn into giant functional ornate mirrors that not even the queen can yet afford.

TELEVISION IN BED/TELEVISION BEDS

Again, this is fine as long as the TV isn't too high up from your eye level. It is generally better to use an iPad for any night viewing though, as you can hold it up close to your face and pretend you are in the cinema. There are some beds with televisions that come out of them but we do not recommend these. This is because we imagine the mechanism of the television emerging then descending into the bed would most likely be more entertaining than the television itself and you are likely to repeat that all night. Doing so may even cause you to envy the television as it gets much more up-and-down action at night than you do. Not only that, but imagine if it broke half-way up or down – disaster!

THE COLLECTIVE NOUNS OF THE ALCOHOLS

There will be times in your life when you will find that you require a number of the same drink at one time. This may be because you are on a pub crawl with friends or because you are a supply teacher who has lost control of their class. Whatever the reason, it is always worth knowing the collective noun for your or your party's drink of choice. For which supply we have included the list below.

A jubilance of reds
A feud of whites
A truce of rosés
A sparkle of Champagnes
A ruckus of ciders
A gag of Sambucas
A trip of Absinthes
A pester of real ales
A water bed of Guinnesses
A sulk of gins

A priority of vodkas

A flash mob of Tequilas

A diversion of brandies

A séance of Bloody Marys

A slash of lagers

A mince of sherries

A phase of rums

A baulk of Ouzos

A parley of shandies

A rewind of Babychams

A lullaby of Amarettos

An unlikelihood of Camparis

A twat of whiskies

A tsunami of Long Island Iced Teas

THE GARDEN

Having a good garden is effectively like having an extra room in the warmer months with really tall ceilings. A garden can be sat in, or stared at, or sat in and stared at simultaneously. Having the space for a garden is one thing but having the time to maintain it is another. If your garden is so big that you can't stand at one end of it and throw a tennis ball from one end to the other then you either need to up your throwing technique, or hire a gardener.

A good gardener will not only keep things tidy out there, but will also synchronise flora and fauna such that there is always something in bloom, like a really slow and really safe fireworks display that lasts an entire year. A good gardener will also propagate plants which, if you wish, you can put outside your home with prices on for people who walk past.

THINGS YOU SHOULD DO AS CHEAPLY AS POSSIBLE

If you are ever asked to write a guide-to-life book with your partner, *never* have a heading about things you should do as cheaply as possible. Doing so will result in a row. The following list has had things added to and removed from it at about the same rate a supermarket trolley has luxury items placed in it by the profligate member of the relationship and removed by the more money-conscious one (with this list it was the other way round, however, in that Frugal MacDougal was adding to the list and Sally Spendthrift was taking stuff off). So, after much deliberation, here is what remains on the list:

Paracetamol

Tonic water

THINGS YOU SHOULD SPARE NO EXPENSE ON

It is important to search for bargains while shopping for anything. However, here is a list of items you really shouldn't hold back on when it comes to price:

Curtains

Fabric fittings

A tailor-made suit (one)

Jewels (these will beef up your outfit so effectively that you could be decked out in a seriously low-cost outfit and still look amazing)

Valentino dress (these are the price of a small car but include this provided that, on seeing you in the dress, your partner gets an erection so untameable that he is unable to stand up in the shop for a full twenty minutes)

VODKA

This is commonly known as 'the slapper of the drinks cabinet', largely because it will go with anything. Vodka is often the 'go to' drink for anyone out for an evening, as it tends to reward loyalty by keeping the imbiber livelier than other spirits would.

FACT: Vodka can be made from anything sweet. It can even be made from milk (which has sugars in it). Milk vodka is actually very pleasant as a drink despite sounding like an alcopop aimed at four-year-olds.

WAITER ATTENTION

Not to be confused with 'water retention' poor waiter attention is something most of us will have suffered during our lives. Surprisingly, it is not waiter under-attention that causes the most stress, even though it can be severely frustrating when you see a couple, who arrive after you, tuck into their tiramisu while you're both still on your soup. It is, in fact, waiter 'over'-attention that causes the highest stress levels in restaurant patrons. An over-attentive waiter will wait until you are at a crucial stage of your anecdote before honing in on your table to top up your water or to double-check with you that your bread is the 'right shape'. Over-attentive waiters are a scourge and are best ignored entirely. This may seem cruel or pompous at face value but it is important to remember that they simply aren't as important as you or your story and that's just the way it is.

WATER

Water should preferably come from a bottle with the letters 'Evian' on it. If this is unavailable then tap water is fine, provided the tap in question is attached to a spring with the words 'Evian' on it.

POSH DINING ETIQUETTE

Dining at a black-tie event or eating in a high-end establishment can often seem daunting. Yet, provided you are courteous and do not slump over your plate shovelling food in like an orang-utan (or any of the big apes), you should make it through the ordeal socially unscathed. Getting through with flying colours is another thing entirely, however. This is because, in the past, posh people invented hidden dining rules that only they would know, so that they could stealthily detect any unrefined diners they were sitting at meat with. These simple rules are well worth noting as following them will ensure not even the harshest of dinnertime despots will be able to diss you.

CUTLERY

The vast array of cutlery should be taken from the outside-in for each course. Before you congratulate yourself on already knowing this, we must stress that almost everyone else does too. This is intermediate 'posh dining etiquette'. So strap in; things are about to get more complicated . . .

BREAD

Never use the knife to slice the roll of bread you
are given. This will be frowned upon. Instead
you should break the bread with your hands
into bite-sized pieces (which is where the phrase
'break bread' comes from. Well, that and
the Bible but we're just splitting hairs now).
The knife is for your butter (and marmalade if
you are breakfasting).

BUTTER

The amount you require should be selected using the
knife and placed on your side plate. You will then be
able to help yourself from there. Don't go directly from
butter dish to bread unless you want any posh people
watching to think you have a cloth cap and banjo and
still throw stones at the moon.

ASPARAGUS

Always leave the last inch of asparagus. This should be
the stump part. If you've left the head part then you
have got it the wrong way round but try not to draw
attention to this.

ASPARAGUS WEE

Everybody at the dinner table knows that eating asparagus makes their wee smell of asparagus. They also know about that whole 'Sugar Puffs thing'. Bringing either fact up at the table will make people think you drink from an oversized Sports Direct mug in your home.

FORK

Always hold this in your left hand with the tines (prongs) facing down, and it should be accompanied by a knife in the right hand other than in certain circumstances (see *Certain Fork Circumstances*). Anything you wish to eat should be prodded onto the fork or pushed onto the back of the fork. Keep the prongs down when eating unless you want posh onlookers to wrongly assume you probably refer to ketchup as 'red sauce'.

KNIFE

The knife is for cutting only. Never eat off the knife. Never eat off the knife. Never eat off the knife. And never hold like a pencil.

CERTAIN FORK CIRCUMSTANCES

Some pastas and desserts will allow the use of the

fork without the knife. Whenever the knife is on the substitute's bench, the fork should be used with the right hand and the law about ensuring the tines of the fork are down is instantly relaxed. You are now permitted to eat using the scooping motion. Marvellous!

BURPING

In the same way that anyone shooting someone with a 12 bore shotgun should hand over their gun to the recipient and retire forever, anyone burping at the table must retire from fine dining for eternity.

PUDDING CUTLERY

The rule for pudding cutlery is very simple: 'Hold the spoon in the right hand but don't use it as a knife; hold the fork in the left unless losing the spoon; if the spoon is retired then it's fork in the right, and NEVER USE JUST A SPOON!

Parents, Pals and Pets
How to Survive One's Loved Ones

The old adage 'you can't choose your family' may indeed be true . . . but you can choose whether or not to add to it. Getting to decide if a couple or more little people get to come into the world or not makes you quite powerful, like a prefect monitoring a school door on a rainy break. Yet with great power comes great responsibility and once they're in, they are in all right. There is no going back. On the upside, of course, you'll fall in love with them and wherever they are . . . so too will be your home. Friends on the other hand are a right pain in the arse. No, of course they're not. Friends are like cocktails actually. Each is a unique concoction made in a certain way – and you're f*cked if you have too many of them. So let's raise a friend as we give you the low-down on family life and cocktails.

– Dom

ARGUING WITH MINORS

Not to be confused with an aspect of Thatcherism, the act of arguing with minors is the art of debating with junior members of the family until they no longer pose a threat to your status. The outcome of this event depends upon the age of who you are rowing with. Generally, anywhere up to the age of four is considered safe ground and provided you are fairly articulate you should win most arguments at this level. From the age of five onwards, however, you are most likely to suffer upshots ranging from 'mild humiliation' to 'total humiliation and headlock'. For this reason we recommend you do not argue with minors.

ATTENDING BIRTHS

Since the 1970s there has been a surge in the percentage of fathers choosing or being forced to be to be present at the birth of their children. The percentage of women choosing to be present at the birth of their children has remained roughly the same. For expectant fathers prior to 1970, standard procedure was to remain drunk and upbeat in either a pub or club, depending on his circumstances. On learning via a pay phone that the birth had been

successfully completed, the man would proceed to
be drunk-driven to the hospital by another pub/club
patron, despite nobody knowing where it was. He
would then eventually arrive, only to be informed that
his wife had already been discharged.

Attending a birth as a man can be a beautiful or
disturbing experience, depending on which side of the
screen you place yourself. The experience differs greatly
in the same way the films *True Romance* and *Alien*
do. The former being much less gory and petrifying
than the latter but including way more expletives.
We recommend staying at the *True Romance* end and
bringing some sort of distraction for the many hours
of labour (see *Back to Backgammon*).

BATHROOM QUEUE

The last time either of us had to queue for the
bathroom, sun factors only went up to eight and
Gillette only did razors with one blade. So you're on
your own here again, we're afraid.

BEING HONEST ABOUT FRIENDS' RELATIONSHIPS

Everybody experiences blind spots, particularly in their
love life, and there will be occasions when the actions

of your close friends draw some level of concern. Even if a friend has started going out with one of the blue things from *Avatar*, you must ask yourself, 'What advantage is there in me calling this?' If the advantage isn't there then it is better to let them get on with it.

BEING MOCKED BY YOUR OWN CHILD

This should always be encouraged. It doesn't matter that you are the butt of the joke. The important thing is that everyone is laughing, which is good for everyone; when you find yourself in the grip of family ridicule just feel happy to be part of the fun. Even if your daughter starts calling you 'Terra' because Alan Carr said on TV that in your wedding photo the frill on your dress made you look like something out of *Jurassic Park* (e.g. a bloody pterodactyl), just enjoy it. It won't stick . . . Nicknames never do. It won't stick right? Right.

BESPOKE FAMILY TRADITIONS

Try to have a few of these if you do not already. They should be upbeat and easy to carry out. For instance, the giving of a wrapped potato every Christmas can be deeply amusing, particularly if you forget it is going to happen each year.

BOARDING SCHOOL

Sending your children off to boarding school is a little like having a remote control for them. They are still in your lives but you get to turn the volume down for a while. Boarding schools are good for the following reasons: a) they teach children to be responsible for themselves, b) they are filled with teachers who love to teach, c) children learn to tolerate and even get along with people they can't stand and, d) anyone who goes, then gets revenge by sending their own children there, which is effectively like paying into a savings account but with tranquillity instead of money.

BREAKFAST

It is possibly more important to eat your breakfast in your bed than it is to actually sleep in your bed. The sensation of moving seamlessly from sleep to food is difficult to beat but, of course, cannot be experienced by everyone in the household (as somebody has to be up to make it). For this reason we recommend you run a hotel, complete with its own top-rate breakfast chef.

CAESAREAN SECTION

The Caesarean method of birth has increased in

popularity along with its salad namesake (the two are connected in name only as it is illegal to ask for romaine lettuce and croutons while enduring any period of labour). Many believe the 'Caesar' delivery method is popular due to its relative effortlessness, but the real reason it is favoured is because 'Caesarean Section' is far less embarrassing to say than 'Vaginal Birth'. Of course the decision should primarily be dictated by what is safe for the baby. Should you find yourself in the Caesarean camp, it is important to try to experience the birth as much as you can. Taking an iPad in with Netflix on it is not a good idea, no matter how deep you are into your series.

CATS

In 'feline only' households, cats are fascinating members of the family who possess really interesting personalities. In canine–feline households, however, the cat's status is lowered from 'centre of attention' to 'mute interloper'. In the latter setup, the cat will only receive attention if it tries to eat food out of the dog's bowl. This attention usually takes the form of a stern 'No!' This is so common an occurrence that many cats in canine–feline households believe 'No' is their actual name.

CHILDHOOD MYTHS AND THEIR ADULT EQUIVALENT

In the past the imaginary characters of childhood would still be firmly believed in by children of ages up to ten and eleven. Nowadays they disappear quicker than support characters in a slasher film, with Father Christmas hanging on the longest before being decapitated by the chainsaw of common sense. This is possibly because it is more important to keep children safe from harm than have them believe their Easter eggs are delivered by a massive rabbit. Regardless of when it happens, you will at some stage need to be on hand to pick up the pieces when they learn these beings are not real. When counselling your children in such matters it may help to inform them that each dispelled Apocrypha actually has an equivalent existence in the real world, as the following information illustrates:

BOGEYMAN

Petrifying amalgamation with many eyes and legs used

to scare children into good behaviour.
ADULT equivalent: The police.

EASTER BUNNY
Challenging fellow who leaves much-sought-after items hidden around home.
ADULT equivalent: Memory loss.

FATHER CHRISTMAS
Largely unseen being, running performance-driven bonus incentives among all those in his charge.
ADULT equivalent: Area manager.

JACK FROST
Mischievous creature who transforms everything he touches overnight such that the gardens and streets of every town and village are almost unrecognisable.
ADULT equivalent: A fox.

SANDMAN
Benevolent spirit who brings good dreams to people the world over.
ADULT equivalent: Vodka.

TOOTH FAIRY

Tiny winged being who helps children cope with recent dental trauma by leaving them cash rewards. **ADULT** equivalent: Injury lawyers.

DRINKING GAMES

Anything that combines forced fun with binge drinking is not going to end well. This is because DRINKING IS NOT A GAME. Drinking is a cultivated pastime which, if done properly, can make various aspects of life indeed more pleasurable. In the instance of drinking games, however, the alcohol is only there to make the hellishness of playing a drinking game more bearable. There is one drinking game, though, that we recommend; it's called 'Let's all have a conversation'. Here are the rules.

1. The players gather in a public house; one of them nominates themselves as the 'Round Buyer' and goes to the bar for the drinks.
2. When everyone has their drinks, they sit at a table and the game begins.
3. Everyone chatters about whatever they wish to chat about; this will usually be something inane.
4. When the drinks are finished, someone else is nominated to go to the bar to get more drinks.
5. Everyone chatters about whatever they wish to chat about; this is usually something semi-serious.
6. The game ends when the barman rings a bell.

FAMILY CREST

Heraldry is as seriously important as it was in the Middle Ages. Of course noblemen no longer fight alongside commoners in battle with their faces concealed by massive visors, so nowadays heraldry doesn't determine whether or not someone sticks a halberd into your body. Heraldry was seriously important in the Middle Ages. Okay, so it's obviously NOT as important these days but it can still be fun.

We don't recommend you have an actual family crest, unless it has been handed down through the ages. Anyone who has been to a museum gift shop and glumly rotated the key-ring rack with crests on will know that finding the one with your surname is disappointing. It is usually just an eagle wigging out under a crescent or some such. For this reason it is good fun to make up your own family crest. In fact let's take a break in which we can all go and do that now. So, onto a shield, draw anything you think best represents your family.

Ours would be a vodka Red Bull and a Baileys on opposite sides of a scale. Underneath, in Latin, would be the Parker family motto: '*Suit et mensam ascendit pannicuols polire*' (Put the turd on the table and polish it).

However this will never happen! Unless you're required to have the modern equivalent, which is a logo.

FAMILY GATHERINGS

Family gatherings (e.g. gatherings that involve members of BOTH sides of a married couple's family) are important for two reasons. The first is that these help cultivate lasting bonds between both houses which will enrich family life in the bigger picture. The second is because everyone is in the same room together; you get to keep an eye on them. Since families differ in so many ways, organising gatherings can be unnerving. For example, it may become woefully apparent that your family is not as big as your partner's and that the voice of your people is drowned out in the crowd of your partner's people. Similarly, they may be just as scared of a smaller more tightly knit family who know more about each other etc.

Of course there will be a lot of common ground and both families will already share similar socioeconomic values. If this is not the case then you have probably messed up. If, for example, you were from a family of astrologers and dentists with a penchant for travel and, on moving to the next stage of your relationship with your partner, you went to meet their family, only to learn they had no teeth or passports and still threw stones at the moon, then it would be unwise of you not to conclude 'this probably won't work out'.

If, however, the individuals from either side eventually discover things they have in common with each other, this will eventually unite the families. Those who enjoy a drink will be bonded not just by their love of a tipple but by their amusement at those in both families who do not. Other shared interests that unite members of both families are sport, horticulture, word pedantry and deafness.

FAMILY PHOTOS

Thankfully these have become less fashionable than ra-ra skirts and corkscrew perms. Family portraits are generally thought to be counterproductive; largely because from the instant they are taken there is always a more up-to-date upgrade available. For anyone insisting on a family photo, do not do any of the following: a) wear the same outfit as each other, b) line up from tallest to shortest with a hand on your family member's shoulder, c) attempt to leap into the air when the photo is taken, and d) have a family photo.

GOOD CONVERSATION

There are of course no rules for ensuring conversation is good, since good conversation by its very nature must be spontaneous. If we were all following a set of rules things would get dull very quickly. You, rather, need some ingredients for a good chat. And they are as follows:

Ingredients for a good conversation

A sense of brevity

The need to surprise*

Wine (optional)

One or more other people to talk to (optional)+

A place where you can talk comfortably unhindered

The environment for a good conversation is important. Make sure you are somewhere you can speak freely and be heard without offending anyone nearby. If you are going to have the whole 'How often do you daydream about sex?' conversation then it would be good to check if anyone is in earshot.

If you discover someone is within audio range of you, and your friends are effing and blinding to each other, it is important to apologise to the person in question, then either cool things down or move away. If they fail to accept your apology, however, and instead opt to look away aloofly like a camel, then just ignore them, but make a mental note to allude to their camel-faced reaction to your swearing in the next book you write.

*Good conversation relies on surprise and humour; this is often why, when with those you are most comfortable with, there is a tendency for chats to be on the bawdy side. There is nothing wrong with this; you are merely throwing your conversational partner slip catches to keep them on their toes. E.g.: So how often do you daydream about sex then?
+ Interestingly, you do not necessarily need other people to have a good conversation; in fact a jolly good natter with yourself is often one of the most rewarding conversations, provided you surprise yourself from time to time. However, an answer to said question is not actually required!

GULF WARDROBE

This is the opposite of Wardrobe Tombola (see *Wardrobe Tombola*) and a dressing approach commonly favoured by females. Instead of floundering blindly for garments, the dresser will gaze into the chasm of her panoply wracked with indecision for eternity, in just the same way that teenagers will a fridge.

HEADS OF THE HOUSEHOLD

Some family members wrongly vie for this position persistently, in the same way that various would-be regents do in the popular HBO series *Game of Thrones*. For anyone at such loggerheads it is important to remember that there are *two* positions of power available in any one household. These are the person in charge of the 'castle' and the person in charge of the 'country'. The person in charge of the castle will be responsible for all of the following: a) the castle, b) who is allowed into the castle, c) who is allowed out of the castle, d) the castle budget, e) castle furnishings, f) castle deliveries, g) knowing all castle dwellers, birthdays, likes, dislikes, collar size. The person in charge of the country is, on the other hand, in charge of: a) bill paying, b) killing stuff, and c) garbage.

It is important to note, however, that both roles are not gender orientated but instead are awarded by personality. Moreover, the castle and country bosses are, by default, each other's deputies so should be able to step into the other's role at any moment. Country/castle meetings should be held whenever something in either boss's remit is deemed 'Too bloody big' for them to deal with on their own.

HOME CARRIER BAG DISPENSERS

The most pointless invention since the wine stopper. There is no point in having a device on the back of your door that scrunches up your carrier bags when you have a perfectly operative bottom kitchen drawer.

HOUSE-TRAINING PETS

This is like trying to potty-train a Chinese toddler, while not having the faintest grasp of Mandarin. The trick is to speak clearly and calmly to your pet while it is getting things wrong. There is also a lot of pointing. Many people revert to placing the pet's nose in its own recent excrement as an effective training method; if you are going to do this, however, make sure your pet is canine or feline and not a parakeet. The process of house-training pets is extremely repetitive so it helps to imagine yourself in a house-training montage, pulling sad faces and sighing while upbeat music is playing. We highly recommend training a pet to ring a pull-cord bell whenever it needs to go outside, provided you have the facilities for this, and by facilities we mean a pull-cord bell and about four years.

NOTE: If you are the first person to witness any form of dog mess indoors, you are permitted to ignore it entirely and head back up to bed, laughing hysterically at the thought of someone else having to deal with it.

HOW TO WIN AT CHARADES

You may not think you are particularly good at the age-old mime contest, charades. But there's a simple trick that will ensure you win every time. The secret is this. Have a bloody laugh with it! You do not win at charades by guessing/successfully miming the most charades. You win at charades by making people almost die laughing at your graphic attempt to silently convey the A. A. Milne classic children's book *Winnie the Pooh*.

Remember, silliness is key, so always head in that direction. For example, if you are doing *E.T.*, instead of going through the alphabet towards E, pretend instead you are on an 'E', off your face at a rave. Don't point at a cup of tea for the T either; mime being Mr T instead. You might not score a point but you will probably make them laugh until a little bit of wee comes out (see *Wet Penny*) which, let's face it, is a better way to pass the time.

LEAVING HOME

Many eighteen-year-olds embarking on studies at university may find moving out of the family homestead a stressful and trying ordeal. Well, try going to boarding school when you're seven then! If you had, you'd have found it difficult but you'd have been prepared for university, wouldn't you? Enough said.

LETTER WRITING

Perhaps another casualty of modern times. The handwritten letter has fallen behind more instant media. However, in the same way that music sounds better on vinyl, the words of a loved one land better when you can see their handwriting and hold their letter in your hand.

There is an even stronger case for letter writing as the medium of choice when it comes to writing to a lover. Sexting may have thrown down the gauntlet for bold directness and speed (and you would find yourself frustrated if relying on the postal system to affect correspondence of that nature). However, you cannot smell a text, or perhaps less creepily put, you cannot spray perfume on an SMS, nor can you laminate it and keep it forever in an old leather chest. Whether the recipient is a lover, family or friend, the art of personal letter writing is of course to write as if you were conversing with the person: 'I was sitting here gazing outside at the rain coming down and I thought of you' etc. If you're smiling when you're writing such letters then there is a good chance you are making a respectable job of it.

MAKEUP DOWNGRADING

Anyone with an interest in the military (or just anyone who has watched the 1980s classic Michael Broderick film *War Games*) will know about defence conditions or DEFCONs. These describe five graduated states of military alert to match varying situations (five being the least severe and one being worst). It is much the same with women's makeup. Most women will know the severity of any social situation and will apply more or less makeup accordingly (e.g. DEFCON 5 would be lounging at home in just pants and DEFCON 1 would be meeting Idris Elba). When out and about, however, most women fluctuate between DEFCONs 2 and 3.

It is therefore considered the greatest compliment to a blossoming platonic relationship if the woman raises her DEFCON makeup level for your next meeting. So the next time you meet with a recent female associate, and they rock up looking like they've put their makeup on in a fun house, congratulations! You are well on your way to making a good pal!

NOTE: If they rock up on a lower DEFCON makeup level it does NOT mean they fancy you. It just means you are still creeping them out a bit.*

*Unless you are Idris Elba.

MODERN PARLOUR GAMES

While drinking games originate from hell itself, parlour games are a joy. Indeed, it is entirely permissible to drink (quite a lot if you like) during parlour games as long as the drinking is not integrated into the game itself. Many older parlour games have stood the test of time largely because they can be easily modernised (charades for example). Others need not be changed at all to still be hilarious.

MODERN PARLOUR GAMES (ADVANCED)

While our ancestors have provided us with an abundance of stencils for 'pissing about' in the drawing room, it is important to remember that some of the best parlour games are those which you make up on the spot. One such game that emerged from one of our own sessions with friends is 'Drunken Dragons' Den', the rules of which are below.

DRUNKEN DRAGONS' DEN

Whenever either yourselves or indeed any guests

you are entertaining claim during a drinking session that they have come up with a brilliant business idea, it's then that you must play Drunken Dragons' Den. The rules for which are quite simple and listed hereby.

1. The game begins when the pitcher (person who has the business idea) agrees to test it on the dragons. Immediately the remaining drinkers in the party must fight over which of the dragons they want to be. Note: Up to two Duncan Bannatynes are permitted provided at least one person agrees to be Deborah Meaden.

2. The dragons get into character and argue needlessly before saying, 'Let's welcome them in.' The pitcher then pretends to enter the room, even though in real life they are already in the room.

3. The idea is then pitched, during which the dragons abuse and interrupt the pitcher until they can no longer remember what their idea actually was. Everybody will be shouting over each other at the same time. This is to be encouraged. It is also possible to have two pitchers, as in the following short transcript.

DUNCAN BANNATYNE: Tell us about your product.

STEPH: So, 'Five Pints' is based on Dom's idea and it's all about a nappy. Not a pathetic baby nappy but a really big nappy.

DEB MEADEN: A man nappy?

DUNCAN: DEBORAH, KNOW YOUR PLACE!

STEPH: It's the equivalent of five pairs of pants.

DOM: No, it's gonna hold five—

STEPH (interrupting): —days!

DOM: Argh, you don't even know what you're bloody selling!

STEPH: Oh, I said five days!

DOM: No, it's five PANTS! Yes, that's why they're called five pants . . . because they hold five PINTS of pee, but they are PANTS! Five pints is a milk substitute.

DEB: Milk Pants?

DUNCAN: We've had a bit of a misunderstanding here.

STEPH: I am so sorry Mr Bannatyne.

DOM: FIVE PANTS! Oh piss off you scots bastard!

MORNING PEOPLE

A possibly mythological race of beings who rise at about five-thirty in the morning seeking yoga activities and kippers. These freaks of nature are said to favour cardigans that have never been in fashion and are thought to be able to gaze upon a sunrise without going blind. Morning people are mostly always the product of toilet-training at gunpoint during their infancy.

MORNINGS

It is important to note that the 'morning' is the time of the day when you yourself feel ready to rise and NOT a specific three-hour block of the early daytime beginning at 6 a.m. A morning can be postponed until about 10 p.m. at the latest. Anyone who offers the mock greeting 'Afternoon' or the equally unfunny 'Good evening' should be punched with the same degree of force as the levity of the greeting (see *Morning People*).

MOTHERS-IN-LAW

These steadfast matriarchs have suffered bad press at the hands of seventies club comedians but in reality many of them are really quite nice. Like practically everyone else in their age bracket, mothers-in-law will fixate on something in particular (such as a neighbour's antics or tidiness). One particularly lovely mother-in-law, however, does not like bad grammar, which is why we haz done some poor lexicon hear so what she will see it.

NAMING CHILDREN

Choosing a name for your new-born is less difficult than many people make it. This is because usually the child will give you the name and not the other way round. For this reason there is no need to rush the process, nor feel the name you first give need be permanent. You are giving your baby a name, not a tattoo. So just take your time. Until you get him or her christened that is; then it's as good as a tattoo! So get it right! Here are a few guidelines we believe work when choosing a name for your child.

1. Be relatively traditionalist, it's the best starting point; too many people go out of their way to be unique. This is a bit like painting your kitchen wall purple just because nobody else has. And nobody wants to look at a purple kitchen wall.

2. Choose a name with some wiggle room, e.g. one that your offspring can tweak to his or her taste. E.g. Ian can only be Ian, but Robert can be Bob, Rob, Bobby or Bert.

3. If you do wish your child to be referred to as Bobby, don't get everyone to call them Bobby, because it is sod's law they will change it to Bob.

4. Never consult over a name with family or friends. Invariably someone will say, 'Oh, that's what we called the dog' or 'Milo? Sounds a bit like Biro!' etc.

5. Make sure the name sits well socially in the area you live, e.g. calling someone 'Shaniqua' or 'Ciabatta' won't work in an area where there are more Castles than there are Nando's.

6. Ensure the name is practical – e.g. calling a child 'Avalanche' is a bad idea as you will not be able to shout their name at a ski resort.

NAMING PETS

The best monikers to bestow on animals are those usually given to humans, our favourites being Colin, or Dave. Colin and/or Dave would make great names for any pet, regardless of species or gender. However, should you find yourself furnished with an animal from another clime, it is respectful to give it a name used by the humans of their homeland, e.g. a French sausage dog might be called 'Gigi' or a Somalian rabbit might be 'Ibrahim'.

NICKNAMES

In the same way a baby will give you its name, each of your friends and family and pets will give you their nickname. Good nicknames are like really expensive fine wines (they will change slightly over time and you should never drop them). A good nickname is an evolution and will often be the result of a shift in logic. For example, someone named Oscar who has been subjected to the constant jibe 'You're the only Oscar I know!' would eventually be called 'Rhino' because of the similar soundscape. Family nicknames can be as short as Pickle or as long-winded as 'Bonstrady nestness buccaneer' and make great internet passwords. Or did!

PARKER DAY

It doesn't exist yet but in case we ever do become immortalised by a day it will have to have rules, and all levels of hedonism will need to be dialled up to eleven.

Parker Day Itinerary

1) Wake no earlier than 1 p.m.

2) Kick off with a Bloody Mary

3) Bottle of Champagne

4) Sausage dog piñata in garden containing ingredients for Long Island Iced Tea

5) Long Island Iced Tea

6) Damn good shag in the afternoon

7) Out for dinner and shouting and singing

8) Carriages

9) Shots

10) Mr Sandman

PICNICS

Family mealtimes during which an already high level of existing difficulty has been super-sized by added problems, including wind, cow pats, wasps, irate landowners, gulls, wasps, cattle grids, poor gradients and more wasps. As difficult and inadvisable as trying to trim nose hairs on the Waltzers. Avoidance is the best tactic here.

RETIREMENT PLANS

The only feasible retirement plan is death. It doesn't cost anything and the lie-ins are amazing.

RITES OF PASSAGE

The process of upgrading from childhood to adulthood involves some significant phases. There are too many to mention but some from our shared memory include first kiss, first car, first bra and first shave. Just to reiterate, these moments are from our shared memory and neither of us has achieved all of them separately.

Another significant one many of us remember is our first proper drink. For most, it takes place about the age of fifteen or even younger if you are from a family who deem it sophisticated to allow their tweens a small drop of wine at the table. Or even younger, if you hoover up left over drinks at a party and your brother gives you an olive while you're still carrying a womble about with you. To reiterate, this only happened to one of us. Only one of us had their womble turn into a 'vomble'.

SENIOR FAMILY MEMBERS (CALLING MOBILE)

When contacting an elderly relative on their mobile, it is important to remind them beforehand that their phone eventually stops ringing because their voicemail kicks in and not because you are giving up on them after five rings.

SENIOR FAMILY MEMBERS (TEXTING)

The first digital cellular mobile phones were available to the public in the 1990s. Since then they have been acquired by almost all demographics in the following order: 1) drug dealers, 2) show-offs, 3) sales reps, 4) the general public, 5) school kids, 6) senior citizens, and 7) pets.

Despite trailing the pack by some measure, many elderly people have made big strides with their mobile phones. Some no longer keep them wrapped in tissue in their handbags and many can scroll through their ringtones. In fact most people will at some stage receive an SMS from a senior family member. In the first instances, the message will read something like the following, and will usually be sent in error: 'Fodfvoiqoe234wejpqwejppqijbdfdfRRRRRRRRRRRR RRRRRRRRRRRR'.

Elderly relatives are not to be chastised for accidental messaging, even if the text has made you panic and contact their warden. Instead they are to be encouraged to text because witnessing their learning curve is hugely entertaining. For example, every elderly person who masters texting will experiment with corner-cutting text slang and even emoticons, making them sound like octogenarian hoodies: 'RU still on 4 Bewley Fundraiser Dinner Fri? LOL . . . Gr8 Aunt Joan J'.

SKYPING FAMILY

Like the telephone, Skype is a great way of staying in touch with relatives, with the added advantage of allowing one to judge a) how well they are eating, b) how well they are grooming, and c) how many facial tattoos they have succumbed to since the last Skype call. While moving from telephone to iPad has not changed the mother's role in the ritual of contact with relatives, the father's role has evolved significantly. No longer able to pick a receiver up, say a quick hello and pass the caller onto the mother figure, the father must pop in and out of vision in the background, returning with various items from the garden to show the caller whenever the mother requests this.

STANDING UP TO FAMILIES

There will be times when you consider the treatment your partner endures from his or her family seems completely unacceptable. It is painful to imagine your partner being bullied or ignored or humiliated at the hands of his or her family. Such pain is exacerbated by the fact that you simply cannot tear into the offender as you perhaps normally would, since it would not do to have your partner think you are a psycho for punching their uncle in the balls because he said your partner had 'put on a bit of beef'.

In all cases such as these, it is important to remember that family dynamics are extremely different and your partner's status will be lower in some areas than in others. Some families will, for example, deign it unthinkable not to receive a gift elegantly, whereas the opposing family may gawp in disdain at a carefully selected scarf and say, 'Did you keep the receipt?'

So it is important to keep in mind that your partner might not be offended in the least by that which is making you have to sit on your hands. If you are certain the offence directed at your partner from their family is malevolence-based, then it is important to check your 'dig quotient' before mentioning this.

Your dig quotient is the number of times you are still able to criticise your partner's family within that year. In any relationship anyone's dig quotient will range from once . . . to never.

TALKING ABOUT FRIENDS BEHIND THEIR BACKS

At the risk of sounding woefully pedantic, it is impossible not to discuss friends behind their backs. For example, if your friend George is planning to stay, you will need to say to your partner, 'Oh, by the way, George is planning to stay.' Without this you are heading for the unsavoury consternation of your partner at some point in the not-too-distant future saying, 'What the hell is George doing in our garden?' Of course talking about people behind their backs negatively is a Class A offence. Like a Class A drug it is also probably highly addictive, so once you start being a 'horrid bastard' to someone behind their back, there is a danger you won't be able to stop until it has consumed you entirely.

TEENAGERS

Pretty much literally a cross between an adult and a child, teenagers are the closest thing to mythical beasts in our world. This angst-driven race of beings ensure that all who become one will not be able to pass any saleable advice down to their own teens by upping the ante of completely unacceptable music, clothing and behaviour, with every generation spawned.

TELLING FRIENDS THEY DON'T SMELL LIKE ROSES

If you find yourself subjected to the bad breath or body odour of someone you're not close to, it is not your problem and shouldn't really worry you provided you keep downwind. If, however, the perpetrator is a member of your family or indeed a dear friend then it is your job to tell them. When doing so, be direct but remember kindness. As ever there are right ways and wrong ways to break such news:

Body odour, tactful approach: 'Oh, I do love you, but I've got to tell you, this hot weather we're having is not your armpits' friend.'

Body odour, non-tactful approach: 'Jesus, Robert, have you been baking bread? Your armpits are so bad they're making the clocks go back.'

Bad breath, tactful approach: 'Ooh, you might have a bit of a bad tooth there, Bob. Nothing major but it might be worth getting it checked.'

Bad breath, non-tactful approach: 'Seriously, Bob, it's like Stonehenge in a nuclear winter in your mouth; until you gargle some Listerine you're banned from saying anything that begins with the letter H.'

THE ART OF JOKE TELLING

Nowadays we are able to access a plethora of humour from YouTube and Twitter accounts as well as some very funny television programmes, leaving actual joke telling with a much poorer market share. Indeed, when actual jokes do surface, they arrive via text in written form, so we rarely get to hear them. The art of joke telling remains special, however, and jokes are always at their funniest when they are told among friends. Here are some simple rules:

1) Get into it. Play all the characters in your joke with gusto. Everyone must have an accent even if you're bad at accents.
2) Enjoy the journey of the joke. It's not just about the punchline; people should enjoy how much you are enjoying it.
3) Go off-piste. If the story is amusing everyone, throw in a few diversions; you can always find your way back.

4) Reinvent it every time. Jokes are like snowflakes in that no two tellings will ever be the same; you need to entertain yourself as well as everyone else, don't forget.

5) Laugh at your own joke. We can't recommend this enough. There is nothing more contagious than genuine laughter.

HERE'S AN EXAMPLE OF A GOOD JOKE: This guy goes away to Devon for a hunting and fishing weekend with his chum and they have a stunning weekend, and at the end of the weekend he gets onto the old steam train and slams the door and, clang, gets into his little cubicle, slides down the window and says (posh accent), 'BY THE WAY, GEORGE, JUST GOT TO SAY THAT WAS REALLY ONE OF THE FINEST SPORTING WEEKENDS I'VE HAD FOR YEARS', and all the steam's flowing and all the leather suitcases are piling off the racks, the fishing rods are poking out of the windows. He says, 'THE SALMON WERE JUMPING, THE PHEASANTS WERE FLYING AND THE PARTRIDGES WERE HITTABLE AND, BY THE WAY, YOUR WIFE'S THE BEST SHAG IN THE COUNTY . . . ANYWAY, THANKS AGAIN . . . LOVELY TO SEE YOU.' Slam, up goes the window and he sits down. And there's another chap sitting opposite him puffing on a cigar, reading the paper. He puts the paper down and says, 'Excuse me, I'm so sorry to interrupt, but I couldn't help but overhear, did I you just tell the gentlemen friend of yours that you'd had the most amazing fishing and shooting weekend, and then finished it off by saying that his wife was the best shag in the county?'

And he says, 'YES THAT'S RIGHT . . . THAT'S ABSOLUTELY RIGHT . . . "WELL OF COURSE SHE'S NOT . . . BUT YOU CAN'T BE RUDE, CAN YOU?"'

THE BIG SHOP

This is the much more versatile version of its predecessor 'the weekly shop' (a strictly calendar-based shop now all but extinct due to the pace of modern life). The big shop can take place once a day to once a year, depending on your timeframe or your household's appetite. Generally the big shop is best carried out by two people. One of you will need to place the desired shelved items into the basket, whereas the other must be on hand at the checkout to say, 'Do we really need eighteen magazines?' Big shops should take no more than thirty minutes and should take place in an establishment whose home brand of beans you would happily serve to your parents.

WARDROBE TOMBOLA

Most males of a certain age play wardrobe tombola (and if they do not then they should). Wardrobe tombola is the act of blindly groping into your wardrobe for a shirt, pants, trousers, socks and jumper, and shoes to put on that day. As expected, the outcome can vary considerably. It is possible to entirely luck out and be surprisingly well turned out. On other days, of course, you can look 'random' or 'a complete knob', which is largely the appeal of wardrobe tombola.

YOUR PARTNER'S FAMILY

Before you marry your betrothed, it is important to be mindful of the fact that you are also marrying their family. This is the reality. Learning that there are more than two people in the relationship can be alarming for most couples and in some cases even 'pant-wetting, leave the country' terrifying. However, before you access the British Airways website with uncomfortably warm legs, it is worth remembering that your partner also has to marry your family.

The two families are now effectively vying for the contract of your couplehood. More often than not only one family will win the bid and you will both gravitate towards them in life, with the other family limited to access to you every other weekend. It is much better for everyone that both families end up in a coalition relationship with you as it can be a waste of family life to leave any losing bidder by the wayside. In order to achieve this it is important to organise full family gatherings with the hope of everyone finding as much common ground as possible (see *Family Gatherings*).

ZOMBIE EPIDEMIC

This is an entirely hypothetical phenomenon but one that calls for clarity in action nonetheless. If you do find your neighbourhood overrun with living dead, it's basically best to give up. If television has taught us anything it's that fighting zombies is simply not worth the carrot. Have a damn good shag, then blow each other's heads off. Note, if the shag isn't that good, then hold off the shooting of each other until tomorrow afternoon, say.

Feasts, Functions and a Few Days Away

How to Celebrate Big Days and Holidays

Having an absolute hoot with your wife all year round might be a blast but it does mean a lot of the big days (Christmas, Easter, St Patrick's, Pancake) don't really stand out that much as a result. Our insides think it's been Christmas since Euro '96. So Steph and I tend to treat big occasions like fences at Ascot . . . they've just got to be got over with as much decorum as possible. Like it or not, however, there are days when lunch and a rather nice bottle of pink won't cut it. Days when you have to push the envelope, days when you have to dust off your best hat* and head off to the races. So this bit is all about how to make the most out of them. Right, off we go.

*I should point out that when I say 'best hat' I actually mean my grandfather's hat, which I do actually still wear to the races . . . it's a bloody stupid stove-pipe hat, which is very, very heavy but makes me very, very easy to spot.

— *Dom*

ALL NIGHT WRONG

Some lightweight partygoers labour under the misapprehension that 'all night' constitutes until about 4 a.m. What in fact they are experiencing here is an 'until about 4 a.m. party' and not an all-nighter at all. An all-night party lasts until 10 a.m. at the earliest. Even if the hosts have gone to bed.

BACK TO BACKGAMMON

Take a backgammon set every time you travel abroad. You can break it out during times of serenity and lethargy. Do not buy any of the magnetic versions of this age-old distraction since the pace and competitiveness dictates you will need to snatch counters up readily. Therefore, making backgammon pieces magnetic is effectively 'counter, counterproductive'.

BEING GODPARENTS

This honour comes with what initially seems like a great deal of responsibility but thankfully usually just entails having to give a baby a Silver Stirrup cup. The baby may appear bemused/oblivious to this gift in the first instance. The gift's value will only be learnt in forty years' time when they realise it is perfect for a brandy.

BEST WAY TO LEAVE A PARTY

By far the best way to leave a party is to simply slip away unannounced. And by 'slip away unannounced' we mean 'leave without alerting anybody' and not 'die peacefully in someone's kitchen'. This does not work for small dinner parties!

BIRTHDAYS

As a couple we often have great hope for our birthdays and go out of our way to make the day special for whichever of us is a year older. Of course they tend to be slightly disappointing the older you get but they're still worth going a bit mad for. We recommend you upgrade as many aspects of your partner's big day as possible. Breakfast, for example, would be in bed (obviously . . . it always is, right?). But hello, what's this? A flower in a small vase accompanying the repast? Yes it is. And is that a bottle of Champagne? Most definitely yes.

You should only have a Champagne breakfast, however, if you're willing to write off the entire day together, which is exactly what you should be doing. Heading home after a big swanky lunch and falling in a heap together is usually the order of the day. We each prefer our own birthday more than the other's.

BLACK TIE

This is the most common of 'big do' attires for men. Most guys who don a white tuxedo will look in the mirror and consider themselves a candidate for James Bond, regardless of age, height, weight or race. Some will even make the effort to walk in from the side of the mirror doing gun fingers at their reflection. Of course if a man sees another man in a white tuxedo they immediately think, 'What a prick! You are in the wrong hemisphere!'

CHRISTENINGS

If anyone offers you cake at a christening, fake a cake allergy instantly. Christening cake is the top tier of the baby's parents' wedding cake. So if the parents are traditionalists you are looking at a nine-month-old fruitcake at best.

COMIC RELIEF

This is not a hand job from a comedian. This is always a big event. We always end up giving money. And it's always difficult to hang in there up to the bit where the Vicar of Dibley falls in a puddle.

CRINGE DRINKING

This is the act of suddenly remembering a deed you committed during a heavy night and stiffening with instant self-loathing. The deed will usually be as unfavourable as it is unfathomable, e.g. dancing too erotically, goosing a waiter, throwing your neighbours' wind chimes onto the roof. At the point of recollection the offender will proceed to 'self-bollocking', which can be frightening to anybody observing, as they will confuse the cringe drinker with a genuine shouty crackers madman. To avoid cringe drinking, learn to stay in control during a session by finding your happy level of consumption and staying there.

DRY DOS

Events with no alcohol can easily be survived by not attending events with no alcohol.

FUNERAL CLOTHES

Wear nice bright colours, or at least one nice bright tie or accessory. People will thank you for it.

HEN DOS

Any event which involves all of your girlfriends having

to remortgage their homes just so they can go zorbing in Croatia is a bad idea. Similarly, dressing in themed or matching outfits and whooping your way down the Vegas Strip with massive drinks will make onlookers believe they are watching a remake of *The Krankies Abroad*. If your friends are going to have to remortgage their homes, then at least let them do it over a really posh lunch at Claridges.

HOs (HAT OPPORTUNITIES)

Weddings, christenings, funerals, regattas, races and divorces are all hat opportunities and should be pounced on with alacrity. A good hat for an event is determined by its ducking factor. This is how low you have to duck in it while trying to enter a church. Fascinators should be avoided at all costs!

HOLIDAY FOOD

Some holidaymakers may believe that delicious food while abroad is the way forward. We consider those people deluded. Food on holiday is fuel to keep you alive so you can be on holiday. For this reason it need only be agreeable. Do ensure you are at a resort with more than one restaurant, however, since otherwise, should the food not be to your taste, you won't be able to shop around and will be trapped with something like 'burger' for the entire trip. If you see a restaurant with a Michelin star, avoid it like the plague. You do not need to waste money on rich food. You already have a head full of serotonin as a result of being in the bloody sun all day with a butler and someone you love.

HOLIDAY RAIN

Opinion is divided as to whether an unexpectedly poor climate should affect the enjoyment of a holiday. Opinion is wrong to be divided. Heavy rain, drizzle or a high cloud quotient will ruin the most important moment of your year every time. Anyone who thinks otherwise is either massively deluded or from the very top of Scotland.

The best way to cope with freak holiday weather is to sit yourself indoors and sob consistently. Sleeping bad weather off is not recommended as you will most likely miss the only ten minutes of sun during the entire fortnight. If, during particularly bleak holiday weather, your partner attempts to cheer you up by serving you hot tea in a mankini you are permitted to laugh hysterically provided you steer your mood back to melancholic once this distraction has passed.

IMAGINE MEETING YOURSELVES ON HOLIDAY

When travelling abroad as a couple it is important to remember you are not only an ambassador for your country but for your relationship also. Therefore keep in mind the way you are coming across to others. To this effect, try to cultivate a fairly positive first impression of yourselves, as if, in fact, you were meeting yourselves. Do not exceed a 'fairly positive impression' as doing otherwise might suggest arrogance. For example, if we met ourselves on holiday we'd think ourselves a great deal of fun and probably even do shots with us. However, the next day we'd be, 'Oh, those idiots were a bit much . . . and what *on earth* was he wearing?'

INFINITY POOLS

While these man-made bodies of water are pleasing to the eye they can be an extreme source of embarrassment to the inebriated. For this reason we firmly advise, after raiding a holiday friend's mini bar, that you DO NOT fall out of an infinity pool. This is because, by their very nature, many of them have a ridiculously steep drop which, while hilarious to the rest of your party, will be no fun for yourself. If you do choose to fall out of an infinity pool during your holiday, however, try to make sure nobody is watching it. You will be scarred for life in more ways than one!

INTERNATIONAL EVENTS

One thing that really grates us about being British is our public attendance at international events. When the Americans show up at a summit it's with a fleet of bulletproof cars and bodyguards, as if to say 'Here come the USA.' We, on the other hand, have David Cameron struggling up to the kerb in a Vauxhall Viva. We might as well play the *Steptoe and Son* music over a loudspeaker, just to emphasise our lameness as our PM shuffles in. Bring back Britannia and get some flair and decent cars!

NEW YEAR'S EVE

This is one of the strangest nights of the year; one on which people go 'woo hoo' when internally they are going 'boo hoo'. Also, for some reason, for one night only Britain relaxes its otherwise staunch anti-gropey laws and everyone can grab at each other willy-nilly. On New Year's Eve, holding some mistletoe is like a back-stage pass to Gropesville. As disturbing as heading out

into all that seems, it is nowhere near as bad as staying
in on New Year's Eve. In fact, as a general rule, if you are
ever at home when Jools Holland is on the television, it
means you've massively messed up. The best option is to
go out to someone else's New Year's Eve party and just
get through it. Let them clear up the mess!

ST PATRICK'S DAY

Just as there are other highlighter pen colours besides
yellow, there are other patron saints days besides St
Patrick's, but nobody really bothers with them to
the same extent. For people in Ireland or New York,
St Patrick's day is twenty-four hours of song, green
beer and frivolity, but for the rest of the UK it is the
opportunity to drink the same amount in a pub you
would have gone to anyway except this time you get to
wear a Guinness stove-pipe hat.

SHITHOLE HOTELS

On longer trips involving destinations off the
beaten track, you may find yourself landed in
establishments where upgrading your hotel room
will only make matters worse. For example, a pokey
room with ninety cockroaches and just two bats

dwelling within it is actually *more* desirable than a grand suite with a thousand roaches and more bats than you can shake a selfie stick at. In instances such as these, crying is not permitted, as the creatures on the ceiling will only consider you an easy mark. A tried and tested coping mechanism is to tunelessly belt out the song 'American Pie' at top decibels. This will:

a) Create a distracting challenge (singing 'American Pie' is more difficult than you think).

b) Last for ages due to the length of the song.

c) Deter any bats in the room from having a swoop at you (they despise Don McLean hits, preferring the work of Jethro Tull).

STAG DOS

All prospective stags should read the *Hen Dos* heading, as the information is the same, provided they replace 'Girlfriends' with 'Pals', 'Zorbing' with 'Quad-biking', and *The Krankies Abroad* with 'Reservoir Pricks'.

STREET PARTIES

These are rare, messy, yet overall hugely fun occasions. Sharing a bottle of pink with your neighbours is the peacetime equivalent to the Christmas truce football fraternisation of the First World War. It can be rewarding to mix socially with your neighbours but it is important to stay in control (see *Cringe Drinking*).

TAILS

Aside from dressing as a beefeater or working in the drag industry, wearing tails is as dressy as it will get for most men. The tails jacket has literally two tails on the back of it, which makes it almost the perfect outfit for coming back from the bathroom with some toilet paper sticking out of the back of your trousers, since literally no one will notice. The most likely habitat of tails-wearing men will be at a high-profile wedding.

TALKING BOOKS

A must-have for any vacation. Effectively, just for eight pounds or so, Stephen Fry or someone will come and read to you on the beach. On the beach!

THE FRENCH

We think the French are awesome. God alone knows why we're led to believe we don't like them as a nation.

Individual to individual they are to be adored. Sure, their ferry staff are extremely rude, but then again, so would you be if you were working on a ferry. No, the French are to be applauded for how family orientated they are, as well as for their politeness, respect and table manners.

To get the most out of encountering the French we recommend you make an effort with their language; you will be surprised how forthcoming they can be when you do. If you're unable to learn a bit of French, then meet them halfway by not rocking up over there in a kiss-me-quick hat and going, 'I WANT BEER.' They hate that.

THE PERFECT HOLIDAY

The key ingredients for a good holiday are: privacy (or at least the option of it at any time), agreeable food, sunshine and a butler.* For this reason we recommend The Maldives since a trip there boasts all of the above.

*A butler on holiday may sound like an extravagance, but they come with the booking. Besides, it is like having room service from someone who will soon become your friend. Tip them only once at the end of the holiday but tip them well. It is entirely acceptable to cry when saying goodbye to your butler.

THE PERFECT WEDDING

Many people look back to previous weddings to try and fabricate the perfect wedding of their own. They are looking in the wrong direction. The perfect wedding consists of two people clearly right for each other, so it does not matter what happens during the day. A good couple who can look to the future together is what the day is all about. If that is in place, then the day cannot be ruined, even if it rains heavily, or bad Uncle Dick wears his tie round his head and dry humps one of the catering staff.

VALENTINE'S DAY

Named after a widely recognised third-century martyr whose love for marked-up rose prices, giant impractical cards, and sulking in restaurants with his partner amid other muted couples was so strong he was prepared to give his life for it. What a complete wanky waste of time. If you love them, tell them regularly. Not once a year.

WHITE TIE

White tie is like a resurrected Gandalfy version of black tie (see *Black Tie*); it's a bit more upmarket and well . . . whiter. It is also slightly more formal, and requires a white waistcoat and bow tie. Never wear a red cummerbund. You're not a bloody bullfighter.

CHRISTMAS:
THE PARKERS IN A PEAR TREE

This is our comprehensive guide to how to survive a Kentish Christmas. The most wonderful time of the year is, to our mind . . . BOXING DAY! The reason we love it so much is because, calendar-wise, Boxing Day is literally the furthest you can be from Christmas Day (until they work out how to reverse time, of course, in which case it will then be only a short drive away in a DeLorean). But sadly, before we get to enjoy the magic of Boxing Day, with its lie-in, its less regimented cold-cut meals, and its television you actually get to bloody watch, we're all going to have to survive Christmas, aren't we?

PREPARATION

It starts with the trees. Yes, you read that correctly: 'trees' as in plural of 'tree'. Namely six of them, each for different buildings. If you thought six geese a-laying would produce a lot of unwanted waste, imagine six Douglas firs fouling every surface with their needles!

NOTE to fellow hotel owners: never put an bloody great big noble spruce up outside your entrance. Everyone will expect one the same size every year after; this alone will account for exactly 50 per cent of your yearly water bill as it drinks you out of house and home.

CRACKERS

These are generally viewed as the most essential Christmas non-essential. Leave them out and they'll be missed. This is because they provide instantly splitting paper hats, which is really what makes Christmas lunch different from any other meal (aside from the turkey, pigs in blankets, stupid jumpers and desserts containing harmful metals). Crackers range from extremely cheap to ridiculously priced. Extensive studies reveal that obtaining the former is the way forward, even if it does mean a plastic moustache with a clip so narrow it wouldn't even clip on a cocaine addict's septum. The bad jokes are essential as they bring everyone together with a big groan. Honourable mentions on the cracker spectrum are those that contain a single bell each along with instructions on how to ring out a Christmas carol as a family.

DON'T DECORATE TOO EARLY

Throwing your Christmas decorations up in November is like paying for a speedy boarding pass at an airport; you're only going to be sitting waiting while everyone else gets on board with the festivities, by which time you might want to hang yourself with a boa of your own tinsel (see *Tinsel*).

HOW TO DECORATE A TREE

White lights will make your tree look as elegant as the banks of the Seine in Paris. Coloured ones will make it look like a really shit roller disco, especially if they flash. Don't hang your baubles either . . . just chuck them into the tree. It's a lot of fun but don't leave one bauble lower than all the others, as this may rekindle any uneven testicular fears you may have learnt in childhood (see *Museums*).

NO TIME LIKE THE PRESENT

By which we mean, start buying all your gifts around September, online, making it a not-Christmassy part of the Christmas preparation. We have twenty-three people to buy presents for, all of which fall under the remit of one person (see *Heads of the Household*). Whoever that is, we recommend going for quantity with a tiny bit of quality thrown in. No matter how much you hate gift shopping, remember it is preferable to going 'Sorry, kids, we didn't get you any presents . . . smile at your granny!'

NOTE: If you are the family gift buyer make sure you hide the presents really well prior to the day. This isn't to keep the element of magic and surprise for your children. It is to protect you from a bollocking when it is discovered how much cash you have spent on them.

TINSEL

Tinsel is an anagram for 'LET SIN' and by putting any up you are enabling a Christmas fashion crime to happen in your own home. So don't have tinsel.

TURKEY PUB CRAWL

The acquisition of a turkey is quite an event and one that will require regular liquid refreshment. Basically, buy your bird from the butcher with the highest number of pubs between their shop and your home. Christmas is a time for parties and a turkey pub crawl is always a lot of fun. Punters will soon get to know the dead bird you're lugging from bar top to bar top and may even give it a name (see *Naming Pets*).

ADVENT CALENDARS

Get the ones with chocolate in them. The best are those with chocolates that don't have actual advent calendars attached to them.

MIDNIGHT MASS

Always go to this. It is like a nightclub without the bouncers; seeing the vicar off his conkers is worth the admission price alone. The admission price is of course your own self-esteem as you amble around the crib and ask the statue of Joseph for a double Morgan's spiced and Coke.

THE DAY

Get up as late as the most junior member of your family will allow. Eat some Scottish sausage in a scotch roll with some ginger wine; you will need it. Never be disappointed with any gifts you receive at Christmas. You are making memories, not acquisitions. If the present is really crap, however, remember to tough it out (see *Bad Gift Reception*). Don't ask for 'Nothing at Christmas'. Nothing has become a thing, namely a transparent plastic ball with NOTHING written on it. This is what you will receive if you have asked for nothing. Invite half the world if you can do, family members, close friends and shallow acquaintances, some will arrive early, others late . . . only stop when you have collected the full set. Remember Christmas Day is the one day you must be nice to everyone. Even people you don't get on with.

CHRISTMAS LUNCH
This should take place religiously at the time it always takes place in your family. Everyone else's time for Christmas lunch is wrong unless you are calling it Christmas supper, in which case you have gone too far. Whatever time you do it, try and take in that lovely feeling when everyone sits down together. And enjoy the fact that you can keep an eye on everyone at the same time. You may then proceed to bang on about how chicken is better than turkey, or are we going to have goose next year?

CHRISTMAS SONGS
Festive music must be selected on the grounds of how irritating it is to the most senior male in attendance. For instance, a septuagenarian father will not enjoy The Pogues' 'Fairy Tale in New York', so make sure this is circulated at top whack for most of the day.

CHRISTMAS BOOZE

Generally speaking, you should be drinking ginger wine and mulled wine at the start of the day. You may then dispense with any adjective-preceded wine and move on to wine. You know where you are with wine. Wine.

QUEEN'S SPEECH

Generally you should try to watch this. Even if you find it a bit on the dull side. She'll usually have something nice to say about us all. Always record it, just in case!

PUTTING CHRISTMAS AWAY

If you're anything like us, by this stage you will be waiting for Twelfth Night with the same poised urgency as athletes have for a starting gun. From the moment the sun drops on the fifth of Jan, you should dismantle Christmas as quickly as possible. This is another great reason to throw baubles into the tree when you first decorate it, as they will be easier to retrieve now. Once everything is put away in Ziploc bags, you can pour yourself the last drop of Baileys, sit back and log on to the internet to see how your unwanted gifts are selling on eBay.

Clocking On and Working Out

*How to Survive the Bind of Employment
and Self-improvement*

I imagine pretty few adults work in the job they told everyone they wanted to do when they grew up. If they did then the world would be a much quieter place. Outer space, on the other hand, would be heaving with all those bloody astronauts bobbing about. When I was growing up I wanted to be a lawyer, mainly so I could make pleas for ridiculous sentences, 'eight weeks of community service dressed as a chicken!' Then I saw all the books you had to read and thought there is no way I'm doing that! I read a fair old bit now, which is ironic. Regardless of what profession or level of your current profession you wish to work at, it's usually a good idea to try to be good at it. But it's never quite as simple as that really, is it? And if that wasn't enough, you've got to be in good shape while you're doing it. Never fear, friend; advice is at hand!

– Dom

ASKING FOR A RISE

The best way to do this is to make yourself indispensable. Find some way of getting your boss hooked on the Class A work you do. Perhaps give them their first few hits free. Soon they will need more and more of you. That's when you ask them for a payrise. When asking for a payrise, always be courteous and calm. Expect the answer to be no, but don't show this. Thank them at the end of it either way.

Never leave it too late before asking for a rise. If by then you desperately need money, you will be agitated, and angry even, as by then you might expect it. This will throw you off your guard.

BEAST-DEPENDENT PERSONALITIES

In an office, beast-dependent personalities (or BDPs) are people who have decided they like a certain animal so much they have decided to make it part of their personality. 'Why do I have all these pigs on my desk? Because I'm pig mad me . . . I'm potty about pigs, aren't I, Shazza?' While BDPs are all part of nature's rich tapestry and are only having a bit of fun, it is not a good idea to get involved with a BDP as, should you eventually cohabit and be involved in a house fire, the

BDP will rescue their bespoke animal collection before you every time.

BEING AN INTERVIEWEE

Interviewing someone else for a job is widely considered a 'false courtship', so to ensure a less spurious outline of the candidate's character it is vital to give them gin. The candidate should be observed in their 'more relaxed state'. Should they remain affable and approachable throughout the session then they have passed their 'gin-terview'. However, should they crush your ribs in a bear hug, high-five the butler, or mistake their CV for the world's least generous kebab, then they are probably not right for your team.

BEING BORED

People who say only boring people get bored have clearly never had any kind of job that involves some degree of repetition. That's not to say you should allow work boredom to consume you. If the problem is long term, then do your best to find work more agreeable to you. If the boredom is only temporary, then break the pattern by surprising yourself by shouting out loud something like 'HEN!'

NOTE: Don't shout out 'hen' if your job requires a relative degree of quiet, like working in a library or teaching Tai Chi.

COMPLAINING ABOUT YOUR JOB

It is the law of nature that you complain about your job. However, this act is carried out by people who love their job as well as those who hate them. If you have had jobs in the past that are much worse than the one you are doing, then you're just in the 'I love my job' category by default. If you can't think of a worse job than that which you currently hold then I am afraid you hate your job (see *Hating Your Job*).

CONCENTRATION

It is possible to concentrate for twelve minutes, after which things go downhill. Therefore, if you read at a medium pace, you should be able to read from the last chapter to here without any trouble.

DEALING WITH COLD CALLERS

Say that the person they wish to speak to is dead.

DESK FLAIR

Your office is your work home so treat it like one.
A lone gonk and a picture of Gyles Brandreth
simply won't cut it. They allow more than that in
prison (apart from the Brandreth pic, as it would
be way too erotic). Whatever you are into, let the
world know. Pottery animals, pictures of your kids,
your karate certificate. Anything. Do be mindful not
to have too many of the same toy animals on your
desk, as this may indicate you are a BDP (see *Beast-
Dependent Personalities*).

FREE BAR

Having a free bar at your hotel may be a great move,
particularly if your guests are well-travelled Americans
who only take a few gins at the most. Running a
free bar in England can often be more challenging,
however. When doing so, look out for tell-tale signs
that the venture is working.

For example, if you find a guest passed out on the
landing stairs, who wakes at four o'clock only to find
he is not only locked in the guest house but locked
out of his room, then it may be time to retire the
free bar.

HATING YOUR JOB

While having a happy life is certainly difficult
when you hate your job, it is not impossible.
If you're able to switch off completely when
your job finishes there's a good chance the relative
peace and distraction of not being there will actually
make you so happy it may even seem worth it all.
However, if you are brooding about work outside of
your hours you are effectively not stopping working,
which makes your pay rate a lot lower than it should
be. This is also true if you dream you are in your
workplace while sleeping after a hard day's work in
the workplace.

HOMING FROM WORK

This is the opposite of working from home. This
is the practice of dealing with all of your domestic
issues on company time: shopping, making meal
plans, deciding which drama series to binge on
next. All of these are legitimate homing from work
activities, such that by the time you get home you
will have spare time to go over that important
presentation for work.

HOTEL LAYOUT

Every detail, both major and minor, should be arranged to your own high standards, even if this is violently expensive to achieve. Guests should be furnished with complimentary sherry and whiskey in their rooms, Egyptian cotton sheets, and feather toppers as well as the nylon equivalent for whenever a guest goes 'HELP, I'M ALLERGIC TO DUCK.'

HOW TO LOOK INTELLIGENT AT WORK

The best way to do this is to remember you already are intelligent. Faking intelligence is a risky business. This is because if you feel the need to fake it, then it's probably because you are intimidated by the intelligence around you and it can often go wrong. Don't be. Remember, when you shuffle into your next meeting with someone, whatever it is about, they are probably just as scared of your intellect as you are of theirs. Unless you blow it by failing to speak or write in the correct manner (see *Bad Grammar*).

HOW TO RESIGN

Say you are leaving because you wish to go to Britain

to get married. Replace 'Britain' with another destination if you are already UK-based, and replace 'married' with another transitive verb if you have already tied the knot.

HR

The office police and the hoarders of the secrets every staff member has or will have, HR people know how much you've over-pushed the envelope even better than you do. This responsibility weighs heavily on their minds and makes their default face really beady-eyed and serious. HR people do everything to hide their default face with playful smiles and, in some cases, personalities, but watch for long enough and you will see that mask slip. Always be on your guard!

INSOMNIA

Many people who find themselves unable to sleep seem to think the best thing to do is indeed try to sleep. This is like someone who discovers they are unable to walk through walls attempting to glide ethereally from room to room without using the doors. If you can't sleep, GET UP! Have an Amaretto or hot milk and read something. When you need sleep you'll sleep.

And don't worry about your job the next day either. If Jack Bauer can counter terrorism on zero hours sleep, then you can work on two hours.

INTERNAL OFFICE FLATULENCE

You probably have more chance of winning the Lottery than you have of hearing someone break wind loudly in an office. This is because pretty much everyone there either has a crush on someone within a 30m radius (see *Work Fancies*) or wants a promotion from someone in a 30m radius (see *Office Swots*). So, as such, everyone suffers all office wind internally. The collective sound of everyone's internal stomach wind is not dissimilar to whale song and, on a quiet day, can often be rather beautiful.

INTERVIEWING FOR A JOB

The last time either of us had to interview for a job, Phillip Schofield had dark hair. Therefore . . . no information on this is available here. Sorry!

LAMINATED PASSIVE AGGRESSION

Kitchenette areas in shared offices will often fall foul of printed messages of stifled rage such as 'PLEASE, NO

COFFEE GROUNDS IN THE SINK :)' or 'WILL WHOEVER IS EXPLODING LIVE GREMLINS IN THE MICROWAVE PLEASE GIVE IT A WIPE DOWN AFTERWARDS'. Remember, just because someone laminates something it doesn't make it the law. The people who fly-post these messages should be smoked out and subjected to persistent light ridicule.

MAKING TIME GO FASTER AT WORK

As you have probably worked out by now, to us time is an endangered species. So the thought of anyone trying to kill time is abhorrent to us. Why *on earth* would you want to do that? Just relax and bathe in the hours that loom before you before they are all gone. Oh, and do some shopping online while you're there . . . obviously.

MANAGING STAFF

We always work with the same mantra: be fair, honest and clear. Out of all of these, clear is the easiest one to mess up. Our instructions are usually about as clear as the weather was during our honeymoon, despite us paying top whack for six weeks in a previously proven hot country.

MANAGING YOUR TIME

To best manage your time during any job it is important to list all the tasks you intend to carry out each day. You should then halve the number of tasks, and subtract three. This is the number of tasks you will actually carry out. Even if the initial number of tasks on the list was three.

MAVERICK ADRENALINE EMAILING

At the dawn of electronic mailing, everyone was so blown away by the fact that their message could outrun a postman so easily that they focused on every last bit of the message they were writing. Nowadays emailing is rather humdrum although it is still possible to receive a slight adrenaline rush when receiving one on a smartphone, provided the alert tone is dramatic enough.

One of the dangers of becoming over-familiar with emailing is the reluctance to bother checking what you are sending; even though you know yourself it is really important to proofread important messages before sending them. Many of us are only able to check anything we've sent the moment after we've sent it (using the adrenaline caused by the act of sending without checking as a means of focusing enough to then be able to check it). This almost always never works, even if after a spell check (see *Never Trust Spell Checks*).

MESSY DESK/TIDY DESK

Both of these are absolutely fine so choose whichever suits the way you work best. As long as you know where everything is, then so be it. Generally speaking it's a good idea for your desk to have a gentle flow to it so that things that need actioning don't hang around for too long.

NEVER TRUST SPELL CHECKS

Never do this. Just because all your words no longer have red lines under them doesn't mean they are all angels. Some of them are wrong words in disguise. Moreover, any typos you may have entered will now have become real words, which will really throw the message you are trying to write. For example, imagine you are firing off a friendly email to a customer called John who you already know is on the large side.

You mean to be informal so you decide you'll start with 'Hey John'. However, since the T key is very near the Y key, it is not at all unthinkable to imagine you accidentally type in 'Het John'. You then whizz a quick spell check over your email before firing it off without checking your document, not realising you have greeted your rather large customer with 'Hefty John'.

OFFICE FLAPPERS

These are people who make simple everyday duties seem like herculean tasks. Examples of this are: a) rushing breathlessly into the post room in the hope they've made the post about two hours before the post is due to be collected, b) bursting into the office in Uggs and a massive scarf whenever a bit of snow falls, clutching a bucket of Starbucks coffee and saying they can't feel their face, even though everyone else has made it in with relatively little disruption or face numbness; and c) believing all accounts of reported office illnesses even though almost all of them are sickies (see *Sickie Dos and Don'ts*). Ignore them at all costs; once you wake the beast there is no escape.

OFFICE GOSSIP

As we have explained, honesty and kindness are always the way forward and discretion is also something you should strive for. This would firmly suggest that office (or any other) gossip is something we would never advocate, certainly not outside of work anyway. But come on . . . it's so addictive, right? Plus it momentarily makes you feel really popular and powerful. That makes it a hard one to call. So much so that we are going to go outside for a bit and have a serious chat about it.

Normal service will be resumed shortly.

Hello. Sorry about that. Right, having had a long discussion we have decided that when it comes to gossiping about people at work you should keep your mouth shut, hold your head up high, then race over to the water cooler and frantically download all the dirt you have on everyone NOW!

OFFICE MIMES

A faction of office workers who are capable of conveying the most intimate dramas of their love life to each other while in the presence of workers who they don't wish to be in the know. Try and avoid sitting near these people. There is nothing worse than seeing someone mime 'My affair with Gary is not going well' through peripheral vision. The worst office mimes are by the ones so crap at it they have to actually speak while throwing gossip shapes.

OFFICE SWOTS

People who try to impress their boss have a tough time of it. They get called Brown Nosers or something even worse. Before passing judgement on these people, let us remember that sometimes the only way out of a job you dislike is to travel upwards through the ranks. To do that you will need to work hard and, most of the time, you will need to convince your boss you are working hard too. Of course there are radical factions of office swottery, and yes, some people really do kiss too much boss-butt; some even try and claim credit for the work of others. But all of these people are at least trying to move forward one way or another. So unless you have massive work dreams outside of your current role, the worst thing you can do really is sit still.

OPEN-PLAN OFFICES

We have a non-open-plan office at our hotel. This is largely because it wouldn't really do anyone any good to come down to breakfast only to see us both through a Perspex divide bobbing about on giant balls while we try to balance the accounts. Or would it? However, our offices are quite roomy, and the phrase 'door is always open' can be used literally when describing them as the doors usually are open. But that doesn't mean you can come in. The hinges on our office door haven't been oiled for years. So perhaps that makes us an expert on open-plan offices.

PUNCTUALITY

We are in two camps about the importance of punctuality and, as such, have collated the following information.

Too much is made of punctuality. BECAUSE PUNCTUALITY IS EXTREMELY IMPORTANT. In reality, however, the main thing is that you have 'turned up' for your job or event, and that in itself shows a great level of devotion and commitment. EVEN THOUGH BY BEING LATE YOU ARE EFFECTIVELY SAYING, 'YOU'RE NOT IMPORTANT ENOUGH TO ME SO I AM STEALING FROM YOU.' If you do find you're running late, e.g. ALL THE TIME, it is important to let someone know, SO THEY CAN ALL SLAG

YOU OFF WHILE YOU AREN'T THERE. When you eventually arrive, make sure to pursue any work immediately and with alacrity as this will instantly turn anyone's negative impression of you into a positive one. THEY'LL BE POSITIVE YOU ARE A PAIN IN THE BACKSIDE, DRIFTING THROUGH LIFE NOT GIVING A SHIT ABOUT ANYTHING, LIKE THAT FARTING HOG IN THE *LION KING*. So never worry about punctuality.

RUNNING REALLY LATE

If you find yourself in one of those four-weddings-expletives-types-of-lateness, make sure you sort your hair out above anything else. It is better to arrive naked to your son's cello recital than looking like a scarecrow.

SICKIE DOS AND DON'TS

From time to time, events in your personal life may clash with those of your work life. For example, during the morning of a working day you may find yourself suddenly 'unable to be arsed to go in'. On any such occurrence, taking a sickie may be your best option, unless of course you are self-employed in which case you are only fooling yourself. Here are some Dos and Don'ts to check against before dropping the S bomb.

DO: Make a phone call to the most senior manager. Try to speak to them directly.

DON'T: Text your sickie in. No amount of sad emoticons or repetitive pictures of cartoon poop are going to make your fake illness seem genuine.

DO: Choose a debilitating illness that can be described in one short phrase, e.g. 'a very nasty bug', 'a severe migraine'.

DON'T: Over-describe the illness, or select one that could be inferred as a hangover.

DO: Speak in your normal voice, firmly and confidently.

DON'T: Speak like Emperor Palpatine from *Star Wars*, or revert to fake coughs or dry retches during the call.

DO: If you have a hangover, make sure your boss doesn't know it was darts night last night (or whatever big event it was in the town).

DON'T: Ever pretend to have contracted malaria while working for NATO, just because you got sunburnt on your veranda on your day off.

DO: Apologise once during the call.

DON'T: Persistently apologise as if your absence from the workplace will cause everything in the world to shut down.

DO: Explain you won't be in for the rest of the day.

DON'T: 'Offer to call at lunchtime to let them know if you're feeling better'.

DO: Stay off work for at least three days.

DON'T: Arrive in work the following day eating a Twix and claiming it was just a twenty-four-hour thing.

DO: Claim you are much better on arriving back at work.

DON'T: Walk around the office at a glacial speed, coughing and telling everyone it was touch and go.

STAFF

As an employer, getting to know your staff is essential. In a previous job one of us had a member of staff complain about the impact of work on his leg. When asked to explain what precisely the trouble with the leg was, he answered, 'Well, I've only got one!' Presumably that would have been difficult for him. Especially if he was working in the 'leapy abouty' department. He'd be okay working with us today though because we're pretty sure we don't have a 'leapy abouty' department. Ninety per cent sure anyway.

WORK BANTER

In some jobs, waiting for a shift to end can be like waiting for two pandas to dock each other. Jocularity among colleagues is important as it really passes the time. Before deploying work banter, however, it's important to determine the preferred piss-take level of each of your colleagues, just as you would the desired strengths of their tea. To this end it's worth doing pre-banter research. Seriously, do it! We had a gardener with a limp once who we called 'Skippy' the entire time he was with us, which he was fine with. It was only after he moved we

discovered he'd had polio as a child. He'd worked
for us for six years.

WORK FANCIES

While not everyone in an office will be fancied,
everyone there *will* fancy someone. This is perfectly
normal, since doing so makes work more interesting
and *all* types of work can be made more interesting.
Even if you have the hottest partner in the world and
everyone in your office looks like an Easter Island
statue, you will still fancy the person who looks like
the *hottest* Easter Island statue. It is often a lot of fun
to try to detect other people's office fancies. Some dead
giveaways are women who upgrade their makeup just
before the sandwich man arrives and men who say
'Ooh, you're looking very summery today'.

WORKING FROM HOME

One of the first things to factor in when choosing a
profession is 'Will I, at some stage, get to blag doing
this job from home?' For example, if you're a coal
miner, you can't just phone up the pit and tell your
foreman you're not coming in but not to worry, you'll
spend the day digging downwards into the floor of

your kitchen. Obvious, but true nevertheless. In the past, working from home required no self-grooming or dressing whatsoever, but the advent of Skype has changed all that, since your boss or clients may video-call you without any warning. For this reason, minimal dress and grooming is required, namely just dressing and taking care of the top half of yourself, creating the illusion of a full self just as many of Jim Henson's Muppets do (although we don't recommend having someone below the table working your arms with sticks, because this never looks realistic). When the Skype call comes in, you will be able to conduct your call with your boss professionally, while he or she will be completely unaware that you are stark bollock naked below.

NOTE: Should the doorbell go, don't get up to answer it, even if you are desperate for your Amazon delivery fix (see *Always Have Something Coming in the Post*).

Epilogue

Well, now you see what I have to put up with! Is it any wonder I'm getting a bald spot? You'd be moulting too if you had owners like them. It's like living with Club 18–30 holiday reps! I know what you're thinking, 'Gigi, don't worry, they're getting on . . . they'll be slowing down soon.' Slowing down? If anything they're speeding up! In the old days I'd cope by chewing through a couple of dog toys every week. These days I'm on twenty a day.

Anyway, I hope the book was enjoyable; maybe you even picked up a few tips to lead a more ridiculous life? I wouldn't know. I haven't read the book myself. I'm more of a television dog than a reader. I've eaten a copy of this book but can't recommend the taste. If you want a good-tasting book, go for *Paths of Glory* by Jeffrey Archer.

In the meantime, do come and visit me anytime. Seriously any time you want . . . just book it and get down here. Your visits are all that keep me sane. I'll do my best to keep an eye on these two. I'll need to keep an eye on myself as well of course, since I've heard it said that dogs can be rather unmanageable when they enjoy a taste of fame . . . apparently Lassie was a complete bitch. Now if you'll excuse me, there's a massive beige handbag I have to be inside.

Sniff a lot of lampposts,

Gigi x